Also by Amrinder Arora

Analysis and Design of Algorithms

Cognella Academic Publisher

Nobel Economics: Nobel Economics: 55 Years of
Nobel Prize History - Highlights, Controversies and
Fun Facts

101 Algorithms Questions You Must Know

2nd Edition

by

Amrinder Arora

Department of Computer Science,

The George Washington University

101 Algorithms Questions You Must Know

2nd Edition

Copyright© 2019, Amrinder Arora

Table of Contents

Which Sections to Skip?
Which Ones to Read?

If you are looking for only challenging questions, jump straight to Section 3.

If you need a primer on asymptotic notation, review Section 1.

If you need a primer in basic set theory and series concepts, review Section 0.

If you need to review your data structures knowledge, review Section 2 as well.

Table of Figures

An Accompaniment to

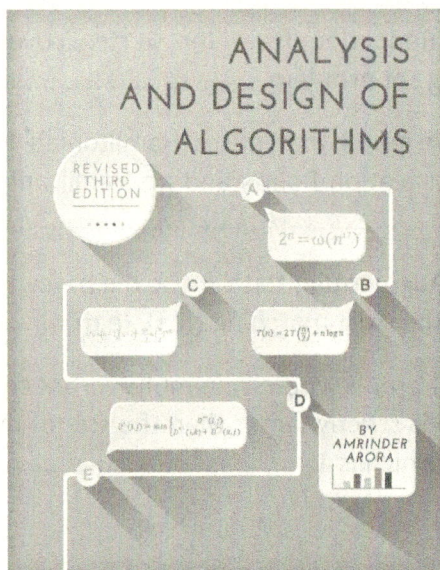

Analysis and Design of Algorithms
(Revised Third Edition)

Amrinder Arora

Cognella Academic Publisher
ISBN: 978-1-7935-2043-2

Acknowledgments

This book would never have been possible if not for the constant prodding by numerous students who simply wanted to get an "official style guide" for the answers to the questions in their algorithms textbook! Many answers now officially collected here in this book have been exchanged with the students and have received their critiques and suggestions.

Special thanks are due to my former classmates and friends Piyush Gupta, Fanchun Jin and Misam Abbas for helpful discussions in shaping this book. Also, thanks to Justo Correas and Jesus Correas, for constantly checking on me about the book, which kept the project going!

Thanks are also due to my parents and my humble and patient wife and kids – Roman, Jessica and Nayan – for their patience in dealing with me while I worked (or at least pretended to work!) on this book.

Section 0: Warm Up Questions

Preliminary Question 1.   Sets Basics

Consider A and B are two sets, such that $|A| = 50$, and $|A - B| = 20$, and $|B| = 85$. Find the value of $|B - A|$.

Solution

We observe that elements of a set A can be place into two disjoint categories – those that are also in B, and those that are not in B. That is,

$$A = (A \cap B) \cup (A-B)$$

Further, since these two categories are disjoint, we also have:

$$|A| = |A \cap B| + |A-B|$$

Since we are given that $|A| = 50$, and $|A - B| = 20$, we have that $|A \cap B| = 30$

Similarly, we can conclude that:

$$|B| = |B \cap A| + |B - A|$$

Therefore, $|B - A| = 85 - 30 = 55$.

Preliminary Question 2.   Log Basics

Given that $log_{10}2 = 0.3010$ and $log_{10}3 = 0.4771$, find the value of $log_6 10$.

Solution

We recollect that $log_b (xy) = log_b x + log_b y$.

Therefore, using $log_{10}2 = 0.3010$ and $log_{10}3 = 0.4771$, we can calculate $log_{10}6 = 0.3010 + 0.4771 = 0.7781$

Further, we note that $log_b a \, log_a b = 1$.

Therefore, $log_6 10 = 1/0.7781 = 1.2851$.

Preliminary Question 3.   Recurrence   Relation and Induction Basics

Given the series $T(n) = T(n-1) + n^2$ and $T(1) = 1$, find a closed-form expression for $T(n)$ using principle of mathematical induction.

Solution

We can get a closed form expression by using principle of mathematical induction. Our claim is that $T(n) = n (n+1) (2n + 1) / 6$.

Base Case

The claim is true for the base case *T(1)*, as *T(1) = 1 = (1 x 2 x 3)/6*.

Induction Hypothesis

Let us suppose our induction hypothesis is true for all values of *n* up to *m*.

That is, *T(n) = n (n+1) (2n + 1)/6*   for all values of *n ≤ m*.

Induction Step

From the given series, we have that *T(m+1) = T(m) + (m+1)²*

That is, *T(m+1) = m (m+1) (2m + 1)/6 + (m+1)*

= (m+1) [m(2m + 1)/6 + (m+1)]

= (m+1) [2m^2 + m + 6m + 6] / 6

= (m+1) [2m^2 + 7m + 6] /6

= (m+1) (m+2) (2m + 3)/6

= (m+1) (m+2) (2(m + 1) + 1)/6

Therefore, by principle of mathematical induction, we conclude that *T(n) = n (n+1) (2n + 1) / 6* for all values of *n ≥ 1*.

Preliminary Question 4.   **Series Sum Basics**

Compute the sum of the following series:

$$\sum_{i=1 \text{ to } n} i\, 2^i$$

Solution

Suppose $S = \sum_{i=1 \text{ to } n} i\, 2^i$

Then S can be written as: $1 \times 2^1 + 2 \times 2^2 + 3 \times 2^3 + \cdots + n \times 2^n$

Such summations can often be simplified and solved using "term sliding".

$$S \quad = \quad 1 \times 2 + 2 \times 2^2 + 3 \times 2^3 + \ldots + n \times 2^n$$

That is, $2S \quad = \quad 1 \times 2^2 + 2 \times 2^3 + 3 \times 2^4 + \ldots + (n-1) \times 2^n + n \times 2^{n+1}$

Subtract the second equation from the first, and we obtain:

$$-S \quad = 1 \times 2 + 1 \times 2^2 + 1 \times 2^3 + \ldots + 1 \times 2^n - n\, 2^{n+1}$$

$$= 2 + 2^2 + 2^3 + \ldots + 2^n - n\, 2^{n+1}$$

$$= 2(1 + 2^1 + 2^2 + \ldots + 2^{n-1}) - n\, 2^{n+1}$$

By using geometric progression, we obtain:

$$-S \quad = 2\,(2^n - 1) - n\, 2^{n+1}$$

Therefore, $S = (n-1) 2^{n+1} + 2$

Preliminary Question 5.   Series Sum Basics – II

What is the sum of the following series:

$$\sum_{i=1 \text{ to } n} i^2 2^i$$

Solution

While we can always use principle of mathematical induction (PMI) to solve these kinds of problems, that requires us to know or guess the solution. If we do not have a good guess, we may need to solve it directly. The good news is that although it is a bit more complicated, like the previous question, this question can also be solved using term sliding.

$$S = 1^2\, 2 + 2^2\, 2^2 + 3^2\, 2^3 + \dots \qquad + n^2\, 2^n$$

$$\rightarrow 2S = 1^2\, 2^2 + 2^2\, 2^3 + 3^2\, 2^4 + \dots + (n-1^2)\, 2^n + n^2\, 2^{n+1}$$

Subtracting the second term from the first one, we obtain that:

$$-S = 1^2\, 2 + (2^2 - 1^2)\, 2^2 + (3^2 - 2^2)\, 2^3 + \dots + (n^2 - (n-1)^2)\, 2^n - n^2\, 2^{n+1}$$

Since $i^2 - (i-1)^2$ can be written as $2i - 1$, we can now write the previous equation as:

$$-S = \sum_{i=1\ to\ n} (2i - 1)\ 2^i - n^2\ 2^{n+1}$$

$$= 2 \sum_{i=1\ to\ n} i\ 2^i - \sum_{i=1\ to\ n} 2^i - n^2\ 2^{n+1}$$

From the previous question, we obtained the following: $\sum_{i=1\ to\ n} i\ 2^i = (n-1)\ 2^{n+1} + 2$

By using the result of the previous question and simplifying, we obtain that:

$$S = n^2\ 2^{n+1} + 2^{n+1} - 2 - (2n-2)\ 2^{n+1} - 4$$

That is,

$$\sum_{i=1\ to\ n} i^2 2^i = (n^2 - 2n + 3)\ 2^{n+1} - 6$$

It is always prudent to validate the series for a few different of *n*. For example, we can confirm that for *n=1*, both sides evaluate to *2*, and for *n=3*, both sides evaluate to *90*.

Preliminary Question 6.   Series Sums Basics – III

Which of the following two terms is larger:
$\sum_{1\ to\ n} i^2$ or $\sum_{1\ to\ n*n} i$

Solution

Both of these terms can be independently solved and compared.

We can observe that: $\sum_{1 \text{ to } n} i^2 = n\ (n+1)\ (2n+1)/6$, while $\sum_{1 \text{ to } n*n} i = n^2\ (n^2+1)/2$.

Thus, the second term is significantly larger for larger values of n.

Preliminary Question 7.   Probability   Basics – Dice, Thrice

What is the probability of rolling three six-sided dice, and getting a different number on each die?

Solution

Many such problems can be solved using counting principles. This specific problem can be restated as follows: when rolling three six-sided dice, what is the total number of combinations, and what is the number of "favorable" combinations, that is, combinations in which there is a different number on each die.

The total number of combinations is *6 × 6 × 6.*

To count the total number of combinations in which there is a different number on each die, we can take the number of combinations for first die (*6*), multiply it by number of combinations on second die (5, excluding the number obtained on the first die), and multiplying it by the number on third die (*4*, excluding the numbers obtained on first and second dies).

Therefore, the probability is *(6 × 5 × 4) / (6 × 6 × 6)*, that is, *5/9*.

Preliminary Question 8. **Probability – Rain and Soccer in Desert**

Antonio has an exciting soccer game coming up. In recent years, it has rained only 5 days each year in the city where they live.

Unfortunately, the weatherwoman has predicted rain for that day. When it actually rains, she correctly forecasts rain 90% of the time. When it doesn't rain, she incorrectly forecasts rain only 10% of the time.

What is the probability that it will rain on the day of Antonio's soccer game?

Solution

Many such questions can be solved using Bayes theorem. A key trick in many such problems to start by writing a notation for different events. Suppose *A* represents the events that it rains, and suppose *B* represents the event that the weather woman predicts rain. For convenience, let us use *A'* to denote the event that it does not rain. Therefore *p(A) + p(A') = 1.*

The question requires us to find *p(A/B)*, that is, the probability that it rains, given that the weatherwoman has predicted rain.

Using Bayes theorem, p(A/B) = p(B/A) p(A)/p(B).

We are given that *p(B/A) = 0.9*, and further that *p(A) = 5/365*

To calculate *p(B)*, we observe that

p(B) = p(B/A) p(A) + p(B/A') p(A')

      *= 0.9 * 5 / 365 + 0.1 * 360/365*

      = 0.111

Therefore, we can obtain that:

*p(B/A) = 0.9 * (5/365) / 0.1111*

      = 0.111

We observe that the probability that it actually rains on Antonio's soccer match is relatively small. This seems counter-intuitive given that the weatherwoman has high accuracy (correctly predicts rain 90% of time and incorrectly predicts rain only 10% of the time), but this apparent anomaly is due to the low base rate – it only rains 5 days on average in Antonio's city anyway.

Section 1: Asymptotic Analysis

Preliminary Definitions

We use the following definitions, that are from the text.

1. We define $O(g(n))$ to be the set of all functions $f(n)$ such that there exist constants n_0 and c such that $0 \leq f(n) \leq c\, g(n)$ for all $n \geq n_0$. (Asymptotic analysis is usually used for positive functions only, so we assume that $f(n) \geq 0$.) We define $\Omega(g(n))$ to be the set of all functions $f(n)$ such that there exist constants n_0 and c such that $f(n) \geq c\, g(n)$ for all $n \geq n_0$. We observe that big omega notation is the inverse of the Big O notation. That is, $f(n) = O(g(n))$ if and only if $g(n) = \Omega(f(n))$.

2. We define $o(g(n))$ to be the set of all functions $f(n)$, such that for every constant $c > 0$, there exists a value of n_0 such that $f(n) \geq c\, g(n)$ for all values of $n \geq n_0$. Similarly, we define small omega ω to be the inverse of small oh notation.

3. We define $f(n) = theta(g(n))$ if and only if $f(n) = O(g(n))$ and $g(n) = O(f(n))$.

Question 1. Time complexity of Repeated Squaring

What is the time complexity of the following program?

```
j = 1
while (j < n) {
   k = 2
   while (k < n) {
      Sum += a[j]*b[k]
      k = k * k
   }
   j++
}
```

Solution

We observe that the outer loop (on counter *j*) just increments one by one. So, that loop runs in $O(n)$ time.

The inner loop runs on counter *k*, and the value of *k* gets squared every time, starting with *2*.

Therefore, the value of *k* jumps from *2*, to *4*, to *16* to *256*. We observe that after *m* iterations of the loop, the value of *k* becomes 2^{2^m}. The loop terminates when the value of k becomes larger or equal to n, that is, $2^{2^m} \geq n$, that is, $m \geq log\ log\ (n)$. Therefore the inner loop runs in $O(log\ log\ n)$ time.

Since the two loops are nested, the entire program runs in $O(n\ log\ log\ n)$ time.

Question 2. Time Complexity with Alternating Big Jumps

What is the time complexity of the following program?

```
j = 1
while (j < n) {
   k = j
   while (k < n) {
     If (k is odd)
         k++
     else
         k += 0.01 * n
   }
   j += 0.1 * n
}
```

Solution

We observe that the outer loop (on counter j) increments by $0.1*n$. So, that loop can only run a constant number of times (at most 10 times) before j exceeds n.

The inner loop runs on counter k, and the value of k gets incremented by 1 if it is odd. After that, it becomes even, and then it increments by $0.01*n$.

Therefore, the value of k increments one time and then jumps by $0.01*n$ next time. Therefore, the inner loop can also run only a constant number of times.

Therefore, the entire program runs in constant, that is, $O(1)$ time.

Question 3. Time Complexity with Repeated Squaring and Half Increment

What is the time complexity of the following program?

```
j = 2
while (j < n) {
  k = 2
  while (k < n) {
    Sum += a[k]*b[k]
    k = k * k
  }
  j += j/2
}
```

Solution

As observed in one of the previous questions, the inner loop runs on counter k, and the value of k gets squared every time, starting with 2.

Therefore, the value of k jumps from 2, to 4, to 16 to 256. We observe that after m iterations of the loop, the value of k becomes 2^{2^m}. The loop terminates when the value of k becomes larger or equal to n, that is, $2^{2^m} \geq n$, that is, $m \geq log\ log\ (n)$. Therefore the inner loop runs in $O(log\ log\ n)$ time.

We observe that the outer loop (on counter j) increments by $j/2$. In other words, after every iteration, the value of j becomes equal to $3j/2$. Therefore, after m steps, the value of loop counter will become $j*1.5^m$. When that value exceeds n, therefore, we have that $m \geq log_{1.5}\ (n)$. That is, the outer loop runs $O(log\ n)$ times.

Since the loops are nested, the entire program runs in constant, that is, $O(log\ n\ log\ log\ n)$ time.

Question 4. Time Complexity with Log Addition

What is the time complexity of the following program?

```
j = 10
while (j < n) {
    j += log (j)
}
```

Solution

We observe that j has to increase from a constant value to n, and in each iteration of the while loop, the value of j increases by at least 1 and by at most $log(n)$. Therefore, clearly, the time complexity of this algorithm has to be between $O(n)$ and $O(n/log\ n)$.

We can solve this breaking the loop into two parts: from 10 to $sqrt(n)$ and from $sqrt(n)$ to n. The first part of the loop cannot take more than $O(sqrt(n))$ time. The second part of the loop does not take more than $O(n/log\ (sqrt(n)))$ time. We observe that $log(sqrt(n)) = ½ \ log(n)$.

Therefore, the total time taken by the algorithm is $O(sqrt(n) + n/log\ n)$, that is, $O(n/log\ n)$.

Question 5. Time Complexity with Square Root Addition

What is the time complexity of the following program?

```
j = 10
while (j < n) {
    j += sqrt (j)
}
```

Solution

We observe that j has to increase from a constant value to n, and in each iteration of the while loop, the value of j increases by at least 1 and by at most $sqrt(n)$. Therefore, clearly, the time complexity of this algorithm has to be between $O(n)$ and $O(sqrt(n))$.

We claim that the time complexity is $O(sqrt(n))$. We can analyze separate phases of the while loop in terms of the value of j.

For the value of j to go from $n/4$ to n, we require at most $n/sqrt(n/4))$, that is $2 \; sqrt(n)$ steps. For the value of j to go from $n/16$ to $n/4$, we require at most $n/4 \; sqrt(n/16)$, that is, $sqrt(n)$ steps. Similarly, for the value of j to go from $n/64$ to $n/16$, we require at most $n/16(sqrt(n/64))$, that is $sqrt(n)/2$ steps.

Therefore, overall, for the value of j to go from 1 to n, we require at most $sqrt(n) \; (2 + 1 + ½ + ¼ + … \;) = 4 \; sqrt(n)$ steps.

Therefore, the total time taken by the algorithm is $O(sqrt(n))$.

Question 6. Sum of Functions

Given $f_1(n) = O(g_1(n))$ and $f_2(n) = O(g_2(n))$, prove that $f_1(n) + f_2(n) = O(g_1(n) + g_2(n))$.

Solution

Since $f_1(n) = O(g_1(n))$, therefore there exist constants c_1 and n_1, such that $f_1(n) \leq c_1 \; g_1(n))$ for all values of $n \geq n_1$.

Similarly, since $f_2(n) = O(g_2(n))$, therefore there exist constants c_2 and n_2, such that $f_2(n) \leq c_2 \, g_2(n))$ for all values of $n \geq n_2$.

From the two choices of n_1 and n_2, we select the larger value, let us call it n_3. Similarly, we select the larger value from c_1 and c_2, let us call it c_3. Therefore, we have:

$f_1(n) \leq c_3 \, g_1(n))$ for all values of $n \geq n_3$

$f_2(n) \leq c_3 \, g_2(n))$ for all values of $n \geq n_3$

Therefore, $f_1(n) + f_2(n) \leq c_3 \, (g_1(n) + g_2(n))$ for all values of $n \geq n_3$.

Therefore, using the definition of O notation, $f_1(n) + f_2(n) = O(g_1(n) + g_2(n))$.

Question 7. Product of Functions

Given $f_1(n) = O(g_1(n))$ and $f_2(n) = O(g_2(n))$, prove that $f_1(n) \, f_2(n) = O(g_1(n) \, g_2(n))$.

Solution

Since $f_1(n) = O(g_1(n))$, therefore there exist constants c_1 and n_1, such that $f_1(n) \leq c_1 \, g_1(n))$ for all values of $n \geq n_1$.

Similarly, since $f_2(n) = O(g_2(n))$, therefore there exist constants c_2 and n_2, such that $f_2(n) \leq c_2\, g_2(n))$ for all values of $n \geq n_2$.

From the two choices of n_1 and n_2, we select the larger value, let us call it n_3. We define a new constant $c_3 = c_1\, c_2$. Therefore, we have:

$f_1(n) \leq c_1\, g_1(n))$ for all values of $n \geq n_3$

$f_2(n) \leq c_2\, g_2(n))$ for all values of $n \geq n_3$

Therefore, $f_1(n)\, f_2(n) \leq c_3\, (g_1(n)\, g_2(n))$ for all values of $n \geq n_3$.

Therefore, using the definition of O notation, $f_1(n)\, f_2(n) = O(g_1(n)\, g_2(n))$.

Question 8. Big O of Small O is Small O?

Given $f(n) = O(g(n))$ and $g(n) = o(h(n))$, prove that $f(n) = o(h(n))$.

Solution

Intuitively, for large values of n, $g(n)$ is much smaller than $h(n)$ and also $f(n)$ is not any larger than $g(n)$. Therefore, for large values of n, $f(n)$ is clearly much smaller than $h(n)$. We can use the definitions to draw the proof more formally.

We need to prove that for every $c_3 > 0$ there exists an n_3 such that $f(n) \leq c_3\, h(n))$ for all values of $n \geq n_3$. To establish this, we first calculate $c_2 = c_3 / c_1$. (Since c_3 and c_1 are both positive, c_2 is positive as well.) Further, since $g(n) = o(h(n))$, therefore there exist constant n_2, for every $c_2 > 0$ such that $g(n) \leq c_2\, h(n))$ for all values of $n \geq n_2$. We define n_3 to be $max\{n_1, n_2\}$.

Now, we can observe that for every $c_3 > 0$ there exists an n_3 such that $g(n) \leq c_2\, h(n))$ and $f(n) \leq c_3\, h(n))$.

Question 9. Trichotomy in Context of Asymptotic Notation

Given two functions $f(n)$ and $g(n)$, both strictly increasing with n, is it possible that $f(n)$ and $g(n)$ cannot be compared asymptotically? Either prove that such two functions can always be compared asymptotically, or give a counter example, such that neither $f(n)$ is in $O(g(n))$ nor is $g(n)$ in $O(f(n))$.

Solution

We can create two functions f and g that use each other in their definitions. We initialize them to 2, that is, $f(0)=2$ and $g(0)=2$.

For $n > 0$:

$f(n) = g(n-1)\text{\textasciicircum}2$ // if n is odd

$f(n) = f(n-1) + 1$ // if n is even

$g(n) = g(n-1) + 1$ // if n is odd

$g(n) = f(n-1)^2$ // if n is even

Here are some sample values:

$f(1) = 4, g(1) = 3$

$f(2) = 5, g(2) = 16$

$f(3) = 256, g(3) = 17$

$f(4) = 257, g(4) = 65536$

From their construction, it is clear that both of them are increasing functions. Also, due to their oscillating nature, neither function can be written as O of the other function.

Question 10. Log of n!

Prove that $log(n!) = theta(n\ log\ n)$.

Solution

We note that in order to prove that $f(n) = theta(g(n))$, we need to prove that that $f(n) = O(g(n))$ and $g(n) = O(f(n))$.

$log(n!) = log\ (1 . 2 . 3 . ... n) \leq log\ (1) + log(2) + log(3) + ... + log(n)$

Therefore, $log(n!) \leq n \log n$

Therefore, clearly $log(n!) = O(n \log n)$, by using values of 1 for both c and n_0 in the standard definition.

Further, we observe that

$log(n!) = log (1 . 2 . 3 . \ldots n) \geq log (n/2) + log(n/2+1) + log(n/2+2) + \ldots + log(n)$

That is,

$log(n!) \geq n/2 \log n/2$, since each term on the right is at least $log(n/2)$

That is,

$log(n!) \geq n/2 \log n - n/2$, since $log(n/2) = log(n) - 1$

$\geq n/4 \log n + n/4 \log n - n/2$
$\geq n/4 \log n + n/2 - n/2$ // for all values of $n \geq 4$, $\log n \geq 2$
$\geq n/4 \log n$ // for all values of $n \geq 4$

Therefore, we have that using values of $c=1/4$ and $n_0=4$, $n \log n = O(log n!)$

Therefore, $log(n!) = theta (n \log n)$.

Question 11. Polynomial vs. Exponential Functions

How do these two functions compare asymptotically: n^{17} and 2^n

Solution

We would like to evaluate $lim\ f(n)/g(n)$ as n tends to infinity. One very helpful tool in evaluating limits is L'Hopital's rule, which states that assuming certain conditions apply, $lim_{n->infinity}\ f(n)/g(n) = lim_{\ n->infinity}\ f'(n)/g'(n)$, where $f'(n)$ and $g'(n)$ represent the first derivatives of functions $f(n)$ and $g(n)$ respectively.

Applying this to our case, we obtain that:

$f'(n) = 17\ n^{16}$ and $g'(n) = 2\wedge n\ ln\ (2)$.

We can repeat this process a few more times (*16* to be precise!), and at that point, we have that:

$lim_{\ n->\ infinity}\ 17! / (2^n\ (ln\ 2)^{17})$ which is obviously *0*.

Since $lim_{n->infinity}\ n^{17}/\ 2^n = 0$, we conclude that $n^{17} = o(2^n)$. As a corollary, we can also derive similar results for other polynomials. For example, the following results are also correct:

- $(n+3)^6 = o(1.05)^n$
- $n^{62} = o(5)^n$
- $n^{62} + 5\ n^{21} = o(1.0001)^n$

Question 12. Polynomial vs. Log Functions Asymptotically

How do these two functions compare asymptotically: n^2 and $(\log n)^{80}$

Solution

We would like to evaluate $\lim_{n \to infinity} f(n)/g(n)$, and we again use the helpful L'Hopital's rule, which states that assuming certain conditions apply, $\lim_{n \to infinity} f(n)/g(n) = \lim_{n \to infinity} f'(n)/g'(n)$, where $f'(n)$ and $g'(n)$ represent the first derivatives of functions $f(n)$ and $g(n)$ respectively.

Applying this to our case, we obtain that:

$f'(n) = 2n$ and $g'(n) = 80 (\log n)^{79}/ n$

Therefore, we have that:

$\lim_{n \to infinity} f(n)/g(n) = \lim_{n \to infinity} 2n^2 /80(\log n)^{79}$

We can repeat this process a few more times (79 to be precise!), and at that point, we have that:

$\lim_{n \to infinity} f(n)/g(n) = 2^{80}n^2 /80!$ which obviously approaches infinity as n tends to infinity.

Since $\lim_{n \to infinity} f(n)/g(n) = infinity$, we conclude that $n^2 = \omega((\log n)^{80})$, or equivalently stated, $(\log n)^{80} = o(n^2)$. This relationship between log functions and polynomial functions is very standard, and all the following results are also correct and can be proved using the same methodology.

- $(log\ (n+1))^6 = o(n^2)$
- $(log\ (n))^{63} = o(n^{1.1})$
- $log^{63}(n) = o(n^{1.1})$ // $log^k(n)$ is the short hand notation for writing $(log(n))^k$
- $(log\ (n + n^2 + n^3))^{2300} + (log\ (n+n^2))^{613} = o(n^{1.0001})$

Question 13. Tale of Two Exponents

How do these two functions compare asymptotically: $(1.05)^n$ and $(1.06)^n$

Solution

While both the functions are exponential, we can easily evaluate $lim_{n->infinity}\ f(n)/g(n)$, which is $lim_{n->infinity}$ $(1.05/1.06)^n$ which is obviously 0, because $1.05 < 1.06$. Therefore, $(1.05)^n = o(1.06)^n$.

The following results are also correct:

- $(sqrt(3))^n = o(2^n)$
- $2^n = o(2.1^n)$
- $2^n = o(4^n)$
- $2^n = o(2^{2n})$ // This is because $2^{2n} = 4^n$

Question 14. An Exponent and Its Square

How do these two functions compare asymptotically: 2^{n^2} and 10^n

Solution

These two functions appear to be difficult to compare, since $2 < 10$, and $n^2 > n$. So, which effect dominates? One way is to simply try a large value of n, such as 100 to obtain a clue. 2^{10000} appears to be much larger than 10^{100}, especially if we consider that 2^{400} is already larger than 10^{100} (since $2^4 > 10$). So, the clue is quite clear that 2^{n^2} is larger than 10^n, but how do we prove the asymptotic *omega* relationship? Once again, we use the limit method.

$$lim_{n\to infinity}\ 10^{\,n}/2^{n^2} = lim_{n\to infinity}\ 10^{\,n}/2^{nn}$$

$$= lim_{n\to infinity}\ (10/2^n)^n$$

$$= 0$$

Therefore, we conclude that $10^n = o(2^{n^2})$.

Question 15. Polynomial vs. Square Root of Exponent

How do these two functions compare asymptotically: n^{100} and $2^{sqrt(n)}$

Solution

All polynomials are smaller than exponents, even when exponent is a square root (or a smaller fraction). Let us prove this using the limit method.

$lim_{n->infinity}\, n^{100}/2^{sqrt(n)}$

Using L'Hopital's rule, we have that

$lim_{n->infinity}\, n^{100}/2^{sqrt(n)}$ = $lim_{n->infinity}\, 100\; n^{99}/((ln\; 2)/2\; sqrt(n))2^{sqrt(n)}$

= $lim_{n->infinity}\, 100\; n^{99.5}/a\; 2^{sqrt(n)}$

// define constant a = (ln 2)/2

= $lim_{n->infinity}\, 100 * 99.5\; n^{99}/a^2\; 2^{sqrt(n)}$

We can see that after a finite number of steps, this limit can be evaluated to be *0*.

Therefore, as expected, we have that $n^{100} = o(2^{sqrt(n)})$.

Question 16. A Bit Bigger and a Bit Smaller

How do these two functions compare asymptotically: $n\; log\; n$ and $n^{1.1}log\; log\; log\; n$

Solution

These two functions appear to be hard to compare due to the following observation: while the first term

$n = o(n^{1.1})$, the other term is $log\ n = \omega(log\ log\ log\ n)$. Therefore, when we multiply these two terms, we cannot reach a conclusion directly.

We can reach a conclusion however, if we simplify the question as follows.

Firstly, we observe that, $log\ n = o(n^{0.1})$. [Hint: We can observe this simply by applying L'Hopital's rule and then taking the limit.]

Therefore, from this, if we multiple by n on both sides, we derive that:

$$n\ log\ n = o(n^{1.1})$$

And of course, we know that $n^{1.1} = o(n^{1.1}log\ log\ log\ n)$.

Therefore, by using transitivity, we reach the conclusion that:

$$n\ log\ n = o(n^{1.1})$$
and
$$n^{1.1} = o(n^{1.1}log\ log\ log\ n).$$

That is,

$$n\ log\ n = o(n^{1.1}\ log\ log\ log\ n).$$

This is a simple yet illustrative example of the value of rule of transitivity, and how it can help us derive asymptotic relationships that may otherwise appear to be challenging. The trick in these cases is to find a convenient "intermediate" term to apply transitivity.

Question 17. Comparing Polynomial with Sum of Logs

How do these functions compare asymptotically: n and $(\log n)^3 + (\log \log n)^4$

Solution

While we can use the limit method and the L'Hopitals rule, it is also convenient to prove this as follows:

$$(\log n)^3 + (\log \log n)^4 = O((\log n)^3 + (\log n)^4)$$

$$= O((\log n)^4)$$

$$= o(n)$$

In this case, the following transitive rule is being used: if $f(n) = O(g(n))$ and $g(n) = o(h(n))$, then $f(n) = o(h(n))$.

Question 18. Polynomial vs. Factorial

How do these functions compare with each other: $n!$ and n^6

Solution

Generally, $n!$ is considered one of the worst (largest) functions in time complexity, with n^n being a good approximation for it, in terms of time complexity. This clearly suggests that $n^6 = o(n!)$. To prove that formally, we can use Stirling's approximation, or calculate the limit directly:

$lim_{n->infinity}\ n^6/n!$ $= lim_{n->infinity}\ n/(n-1)\ n/(n-2)$ $n/(n-3)\ n/(n-4)\ n/(n-5)\ 1/(n-6)!$

$= 0.$ // We note that $lim_{n->infinity}\ n/(n-1) = 1.$

Therefore, $n^6 = o(n!)$

Question 19. Polynomial vs. Combinatorial Expressions

How do these functions compare with each other: $C(n,n/3)$ and n^4

Solution

Like the previous question, we can derive that $n^4 = o(C(n, n/3))$, by noting that $C(n, n/3) = n! / (n/3)!$ $(2n/3)!)$, and therefore, $lim_{n->infinity}\ n^4/C(n,n/3) = 0.$ The result holds even if the value of the exponent (4) is increased to any other constant.

Question 20. Asymptotic Functions with Floors and Ceilings

How do these functions compare with each other: $(ceil\ x)^3$ and $(floor\ x)^4$

Solution

Here, the *ceil(x)* and *floor(x)* refer to the ceiling and floor operators, implying that variable x is a continuous variable here, not integer. To compare these two functions, we observe that $ceil(x) < x + 1$. Similarly, $floor(x) > x - 1$.

We can prove that $(x+1)^3 = o(x-1)^4$ by evaluating the limit as x tends to *infinity*. Then, using transitivity, we observe that $(ceil\ x)^3 = O(x+1)^3 = o(x-1)^4 = O(floor\ x)^4$. Therefore, we can reach the conclusion that $(ceil\ x)^3 = o(floor\ x)^4$.

Section 2: Data Structures, Sorting & Searching

Question 21. Second Largest

Give an efficient algorithm to find the second-largest number among n numbers. You can do better than $2n - 3$ comparisons.

Solution

We note that $2n - 3$ comparisons refer to the number of comparisons that will be needed if first find the largest number (using $n - 1$ comparisons), and then from the remaining $n - 1$ numbers, we find the largest number again (using $n - 2$ comparisons). This simplistic method requires $2n - 3$ comparisons.

However, as the question suggests, we can do better than this. A tennis tournament can be used as our guide to solve this. Given n players, a tennis like tournament can be held with *ceiling($\log_2 n$)* rounds to decide the winner (the best player, or the largest number in term of numbers). While we normally think of the tournament runner up as the second-best player, in terms of numbers, the second largest number can be any of the numbers that lost to (by way of comparison) to the eventual winner. Therefore, if we just find the largest number amongst all the numbers that were compared with the largest numbers, we can find the second largest number in only $n - 1 + ceiling(log_2 n) - 1$, that is $n + ceiling(log_2 n) - 2$ comparisons.

Question 22. Sum of Pair

Given an unsorted list of integers $a_1, a_2, \ldots a_n$, design an algorithm that checks if there is a pair a_i, a_j that adds up to exactly M. The time complexity of your algorithm should be $O(n \log n)$ or better.

Solution

If we were to simply consider all possible pairs, we would evaluate n^2 combinations, and that would require at least $\Omega(n^2)$ time. Instead, we can sort the numbers and compare in a more structured fashion as follows:

Step 1: Sort the numbers, so that $a_1 < a_2 < .. < a_n$

Step 2: Establish two counters: i and j, initialized to values 1 and n respectively.

If $a_i + a_j = M$, then we have found the desired pair.

If $a_i + a_j > M$, then decrement j

If $a_i + a_j < M$, then increment i

If $i > j$, then we conclude that no such pair exists.

Time Complexity Analysis: We observe that the step 1 takes $O(n \log n)$ time by using any sorting algorithm, such as merge sort, etc. The step 2 takes a total of $O(n)$ time, as in each step we increment i or decrement j, and the algorithm stops when i exceeds j.

We can also use an alternate method, in which we use sorting and then use binary search:

```
Sort the array
  for each element a_i in array
    binary search M - a_i
```

As can be easily observed, this alternative method takes $O(n \log n)$ time as well.

Question 23. Three Set Sum

You are given an integer k and 3 sets A, B and C, each containing n numbers. Give an efficient algorithm to determine if there exist 3 integers a, b, c (in sets A, B, C respectively), such that $a + b + c = k$. The time complexity of your algorithm should be $O(n^2)$ or better.

Solution

One way to approach this question is follows. We simply sort all 3 sets A, B and C. This takes $O(n \log n)$ time. Then, for each value a in A, we simply search for the corresponding value (i.e., $k-a$) in sets B and C. As we observed in the previous question, that can be done in $O(n)$ time by iterating on the already sorted sets B and C. The entire process then takes $O(n^2)$ time.

Question 24. Dynamic Median

You are given a stream of integers, and you want to continuously calculate the median of the numbers seen so far. The median is the middle value in an ordered integer list. If the size of the list is even, the median is the average of the two middle numbers.

Design a data structure that supports the following operations efficiently:

1. AddNum(num): Adds a number to the data structure.
2. FindMedian(): Returns the median of all elements so far.

Solution

To efficiently maintain the median of a stream of integers, we can use two heaps: a **Max Heap** to store the smaller half of the numbers and a **Min Heap** to store the larger half. This approach allows us to efficiently keep track of the middle elements as new numbers are added to the stream.

- **Max Heap**: This heap stores the smaller half of the numbers. In a max heap, the root is the largest element of this half.

- **Min Heap**: This heap stores the larger half of the numbers. In a min heap, the root is the smallest element of this half.

The heaps are maintained such that the sizes of the two heaps differ by at most one element. This balance ensures that the median can be easily calculated.

When a new number is added using AddNum(num) method, follow these steps:

1. Insertion: If the number is less than or equal to the root of the Max Heap (or if the Max Heap is empty), we add it to the Max Heap. Otherwise, we add it to the Min Heap.

2. Balancing: After insertion, the sizes of the two heaps might differ by more than one

element. If the Max Heap has more than one extra element compared to the Min Heap, move the root of the Max Heap to the Min Heap. If the Min Heap has more elements than the Max Heap, move the root of the Min Heap to the Max Heap. This balancing ensures the heaps are always nearly equal in size, maintaining the property needed to calculate the median.

Calculating the Median with **FindMedian()**

- If the sizes of the two heaps are equal, the median is the average of the roots of the Max Heap and Min Heap.

- If the Max Heap has one more element than the Min Heap, the median is the root of the Max Heap (since it represents the middle element in an odd-sized list).

Time Complexity

AddNum(num): *O(log n)* — Adding a number to a heap and possibly rebalancing the heaps both take *O(log n)* time.

FindMedian(): *O(1)* — Retrieving the root elements of the heaps (or their average) takes constant time. We note that this operation only retrieves (peeks) at the root elements – it doesn't modify any data structure.

Why Use a Max Heap and Min Heap?

The combination of a Max Heap and Min Heap is effective for this problem because:

Efficient Median Calculation: By splitting the numbers into two halves (the smaller half in the Max Heap and the larger half in the Min Heap), we can efficiently find the median. If the total number of elements is odd, the median is the root of the heap with more elements. If it's even, the median is the average of the roots of both heaps.

Efficient Insertions and Balancing: Heaps provide $O(log\ n)$ time complexity for insertions and removals, which is optimal for dynamically maintaining the two halves of the dataset.

Dynamic Data Stream Handling: As new numbers arrive, the heaps dynamically adjust, maintaining their size properties and allowing for efficient median calculation at any point.

By maintaining these properties and balancing the heaps correctly, this approach allows us to keep track of the median in a dynamic data stream efficiently.

Section 3:   Divide and Conquer

Question 25. Optimality of Merge Routine

Consider the following algorithm to merge two sorted lists. Algorithm simply starts at the head of the two lists, adds the smaller element to the output list and increments the index on the list from which it extracted the element. Can you argue that this algorithm is optimal, that is, there exist two lists that will require these many comparisons? Alternatively, can you find a better merging algorithm?

Solution

This algorithm needs *n-1* comparisons in the worst case, as it always advances at least one element to the merged list (and then the last element joins the list without requiring any comparison).

Using an adversary argument we can prove that this algorithm is optimal in terms of the number of comparisons that it needs. The adversary argument works as follows. We (the algorithm) can compare numbers in any order that we want. The adversary can choose the outcome of each comparison, as long as it does not contradict itself. The adversary can always ensure that only one number enters the merged list, per comparison, with the exception of the last number. Hence, the simple merge algorithm is asymptotically optimal.

Question 26. Probabilistic Quick Select

In the QuickSelect algorithm – probabilistic version, if we define a "good" partition to be such that each partition is at least one-third of the original size, is the resulting algorithm still linear time?

Solution

The time complexity of the probabilistic quick select is given by the recurrence relation:

$T(n) = T(kn) + cn$, where c is the constant to reflect the expected number of times we need to do a partition, and k is the constant to reflect the size of the sublist.

If we define a "good" partition to be such that each partition is at least one-third of the original size, then the probability that a partition is a good partition is $1/3$. Therefore, the expected number of times we need to do a partition is 3. The worst case size of the sublist is $2/3$ of the original list. Therefore, the recurrence relation can be written as:

$T(n) = T(2n/3) + 3n.$

This can be solved to be $T(n) = 9n$, and clearly, this is also linear time.

Question 27. Deterministic Quick Select – Variations

In the QuickSelect algorithm – median of medians version, if we use groups of size 7 instead of size 5, is the resulting algorithm still linear time? Is the resulting algorithm better, or worse? What if we use groups of size 3?

Solution

The time complexity of the deterministic Quick Select algorithm can be written as:

$T(n) = kn + T(n/k) + T(n [1 - (k+1)/4k^2])$, where we use groups of size k, and assuming k is odd.

We can evaluate this for different values of k.

For $k=5$, $T(n) = 5n + T(n/5) + T(7n/10)$

For $k=7$, $T(n) = 7n + T(n/7) + T(5n/7)$

For $k=3$, $T(n) = 3n + T(n/3) + T(2n/3)$

By solving the last recurrence relation, we observe, that when we use partition of size *3*, *T(n) = O(n log n)*, that is, the resulting time is not linear.

Question 28. Binary Search in Special Sequence

You are given a sequence of *n* numbers *A(1), ... , A(n)*, with a very special property, that adjacent numbers are "off" by no more than *1*. For example, here is a valid sequence: *[100, 99, 99, 98, 99, 100, 100, 101, 102, 103, 104, 105, 104, 103, 103, 103, 102]*. Say the first number in the sequence is *x*, the last one is *y*, and you are given a number *z*, such that *x < z < y*. You have to find the location of *z* in the sequence (or report that it does not exist). The time complexity of your algorithm should be *O(log n)* or better.

Solution

Since the given sequence has no "jumps", then clearly, if the first number in the sequence is *x*, the last one is *y*, then, every *z*, such that *x < z < y* must exist in the sequence. To find any *z*, we can simply use binary search. Binary search works, in the following sense, even though the given array is not sorted in the traditional sense.

Suppose we inspect the middle point of the array, and that is a number *w*, such that *z < w*. Then, we argue that *z* must exist in the first half of the array between *x* and *w*.   Similarly, if *w* < *z*, then *z* must exist in the second half of the array between *w* and *y*. This leads to a straight forward binary search like algorithm with recurrence relation of *T(n) = T(n/2) + 1*, and therefore the time complexity of the algorithm is *O(log n)*.

Question 29. Median of Two Sorted Arrays

You are given two sorted arrays *A* and *B* of size *n* and *m* respectively. Find the median of *A U B*. The overall run time complexity of the algorithm should be sub linear.

Solution

For the sake of readability, we use the 1-indexing in the answer below. That is, arrays are: A[1..n] and B[1..m].

Firstly, we observe that if merge the arrays *A* and *B,* then the median can be found directly, but in that case the total time would be *O(n+m)*, that is, linear. So, our interest is in not merging the arrays.

Secondly, we observe that in the edge case that one array is entirely smaller than the other, we can easily find the median by simply computing the index of the median in one of the two arrays. (As an example, if *n = 1000* and *m = 2000* and if *A[n] < B[1]*, then we can simply return *B[500]* as the median.)

Therefore, we assume that the edge case does not apply.

Like many other D&C algorithms, we first generalize the problem so that it returns usual Selection answer, and not just the median. That is, we change the problem definition to:

Selection(A,i1,i2,B,j1,j2,k)

Now, we proceed as follows. Suppose the median of array A is a. Now, we can simply do a binary search for a in array B, in $O(log\ m)$ time. Let us suppose the location of a in array B is z. Then, we have 3 cases like the case of a usual binary search:

- If $(n' + m')/2 < k$: In this case, we can eliminate left-hand portions of the two arrays. Then we can make a recursive call and return *Selection(A,i1+n/2,i2,B,z+1,j2,k – z – n/2)*
- If $n/2 + z = k$, then we can just return a.
- If $n/2 + z > k$, then we can eliminate the right-hand portions of the two arrays, and return
  Selection(A,i1,i2-n/2,B,j1,z,k – m + z – n/2)

We observe that the array A always gets cut in half, while the array B decreases, but not with the same predictability. The time complexity relationship that we obtain is T(n) = T(n/2) + O(log m). This leads to T(n) = O(log n log m).

Question 30. Closest Pair of Points Variation

Consider the "closest pair of points" problem. Suppose we simply sort the points by their x-dimensions in the first step, in *O(n log n)* time instead of using the linear time median finding algorithm. How does this change the time complexity of the entire algorithm?

Solution

If we simply sort the points by their x-dimensions, then the overall recurrence relation becomes:

$$T(n) = O(n \log n) + 2\, T(n/2) + O(n).$$

Using master theorem, we can solve this equation to *T(n) = O(n log²n)*. [We observe that this expression is *O(n log n log n)*, and not *O(n log log n)*.]

Question 31. Finding Frequent Numbers in Linear Time

Given an array of *n* unsorted numbers, give a linear time algorithm to find if there exists a number in the array that exists at least *10%* of the time, that is, at least *n/10* times. (For example, if the array has *1000* elements, a number that appears *100* or more times.)

Solution

This question can be solved using a constant number of invocations of the selection algorithm. We observe that if a number exists at least *n/10* times, it must be a number that is either the smallest number, or *n/10*-th number, *2n/10*-th number in sorted number, etc. Therefore, if we simply use the linear time selection algorithm a total of *11* times, we can then count those elements (also in linear time) and identify if any element appears at least *10%* of the time.

Question 32. Power in Linear Time

Design and implement an algorithm for function *power(integer a, integer n)* that computes a^n, in *O(log n)* time for any value of $n > 0$.

Solution

We use Divide and Conquer to solve this problem, with the basic concept being that of repeated squaring. We use the standard mathematical model where multiplications take *O(1)* time. For example, we observe that we can calculate a^{32} from a^{16} in constant time. We just adjust this idea to take into

account that number n may be odd or even as
follows:

```
power (int a, int n) {
  // base case
  if (n == 1)
    return a

  mid = n/2
  // integer division, returns floor value.
  int previous = power(a,mid);
  // recursive call

  if n%2 == 1
    return previous * previous * a
  else
    return previous * previous
}
```

We observe that the recurrence relation becomes:
$T(n) = T(n/2) + 1$, which of course leads to $O(log\ n)$
time.

Question 33. Probability – 1000 in a Sum of Dice

You roll a standard six faced unbiased dice unlimited
times, and keep your running sum. What is the
probability you will hit 1000 (at some point of time)?

Solution

Suppose *p(n)* represents the probability that we hit *n*
at some point of time. Further, the probability that

the unbiased dice lands on any number (1..6) is presented by $q = 1/6$.

We can articulate this solution by using a recurrence relation for values of $n > 6$:

$$p(n) = p(n-6)\, q + p(n-5)\, q + p(n-4)\, q + \ldots + p(n-1)\, q$$

That is, $p(n)$ is the average of previous six values.

Since initially we start with a sum of 0, we have that $p(0) = 1$. The starting values of this recurrence relation can also be easily calculated as follows:

$$p(1) = q$$

$$p(2) = p(1)\, q + q$$

$$p(3) = p(1)\, q + p(2)\, q + q$$

$$p(4) = p(1)\, q + p(2)\, q + p(3)\, q + q$$

$$p(5) = p(1)\, q + p(2)\, q + p(3)\, q + p(4)\, q + q$$

$$p(6) = p(1)\, q + p(2)\, q + p(3)\, q + p(4)\, q + p(5)\, q + q$$

Therefore, we can calculate empirically (using a program, or by using Excel), the value of $p(n)$ for any value of n. We observe that the series stabilizes to $p(n) = 0.2857$ for large values of n.

We can also observe that the average of numbers on the dice is 3.5, and that $p(n)$ stabilizes to $1/3.5$.

Question 34. An Ancient Problem (Josephus Problem)

Consider n people standing in a circle, marked from 1 to n. Suppose every second standing person is asked to sit down, and this process continues in the circle until only one person is left standing. What is the initial index of the last person left standing?

Solution

We can develop an insight into this problem by using a value of n, which is a power of 2, for example, 16. We observe that in this case, when every second person sits down, 8 people remain, and in subsequent rounds, only 4, and then 2 people remain and finally the first person in the circle is the last person left standing.

Therefore, we have solved this problem for any power of 2. For a value of n that is not a power of 2, we can reduce it to a problem involving power of 2, by first eliminating some people until a power of 2 people remain. For example, suppose we start with 66 people in a circle. When the 2nd and 4th person sit down, we are effectively at 5th person, with 64 (a power of 2) people in circle, and therefore, using our previous argument, the 5th person is the last person left standing. We can generalize that index to $2(n - 2^k) + 1$ where 2^k is the largest power of 2 that is less than or equal to n.

To summarize, the initial index of the last person standing will always be odd. If n is a power of 2, the last person standing will be at index 1. Starting from a power of 2, each time a person is added to the circle, n increases by 1 and the index of the last person standing increases by 2. As an example, if $n = 25$, then, the highest power of 2, $k = 4$, and the initial index of the last person standing is $2(25 - 16) + 1 = 2 * 9 + 1 = 19$.

Question 35. Multiplying complex numbers in 3 multiplications

Consider the problem of multiplying two complex numbers $z_1 = u + iv$ and $z_2 = w + ix$, where the product is $z_1 z_2 = (uw - xv) + i(vw + ux)$. We observe that the product requires 4 multiplications: uw, xv, vw and ux. Can you rewrite this in a way so that it only involves 3 multiplications instead of 4?

Solution

This exercise simply involves rearranging of terms. We observe that:

$$z_1 z_2 = (uw - xv) + i(vw + ux)$$

Also, we observe that:

$$(u + v)(w + x) = uw + vw + ux + vx$$

That is, $(vw + ux) = (u+v)(w+x) - uw - vx$

So, we can write it as $z_1 z_2 = (uw - xv) + i((u+v)(w+x) - uw - xv)$

Therefore using 3 multiplications: uw, xv, $(u+y)(w+x)$, we can calculate $z_1 z_2$

Question 36. Missing Number in Arithmetic Progression

You are given an array that represents elements of arithmetic progression in order. One element is missing in the progression. Give an algorithm to find the missing number. For example, given: *1, 5, 9, 13, 17, 21, 25, 29, 37*, the answer is *33*. Given *n* numbers, your algorithm should take *O(log n)* time.

Solution

We can solve this problem using a straight forward application of binary search. We inspect the middle number and compare that to the expected number in the progression. Based on the results of the comparison, we can discard either the left half or the right half of the array, and therefore, we obtain the familiar *T(n) = T(n/2) + 1* recurrence relation. Therefore, the time complexity is *O(log n)*.

We also observe that the same argument works if the numbers are in geometric progression also, or in any other progression, as long as we can calculate the next element in the progression.

Question 37. Staircase / Pareto-optimal points

Let P be a set of n points in a 2-dimensional plane. A point $p \in P$ is Pareto-optimal if no other point is both above and to the right of p. The sorted sequence of Pareto-optimal points describes a top-right staircase with the interior points of P below and to the left of the staircase. We want to compute this staircase.

1. Suppose the points in P are already given in sorted order from left to right. Describe an algorithm to compute the staircase of P in $O(n)$ time.
2. Describe an algorithm to compute the staircase of P in $O(n \log n)$ time.

Solution

We observe that the right most point of the set P must be on the staircase. By the same logic, the top most point (that is, the point with the largest y-value) must also be on the staircase. Using this observation, we can compute the staircase in $O(n)$ time if we are given the points in P in sorted order. We simply iterate the set of points from right to left, and include every point that has a *y*-value higher than the previously known maximum *y*-value.

The following pseudocode describes the process:

```
ymax = negative_infinity
for point p in P in sorted order from right
to left {
    if p.y > ymax {
        include p in staircase
        ymax = p.y
    }
}
```

Using this observation we can come up with a simple algorithm to compute the staircase in $O(n \log n)$ time. Firstly, we simply sort the points, and then follow the procedure outlined above.

Question 38. Convex Hull

We are given a set P of n points in a two-dimensional plan, and we want to compute the convex hull of P. The convex hull is defined as the smallest convex polygon containing the points. (A way to visualize a convex hull is to imagine nails on all the points of the plane and put an elastic band around the points – the shape of the elastic band is the convex hull.) Describe an $O(n \log n)$ time divide and conquer algorithm to find the convex hull of the set P of n points.

Solution

A simple divide and conquer algorithm simply divides the set of points by using the median in terms of their x-axis. We make two recursive calls on the left hand side and the right hand side, and then combine the two convex hulls. If we merge two convex hulls into one in linear time, then our overall recurrence relation will look as follows:

$$T(n) = 2\ T(n/2) + O(n)$$

Therefore, this question can be equivalently stated as, given two convex hulls, merge them into one in linear time.

To merge two convex hulls, one approach is as follows: find the "east" most point in the left convex hull (that is, the point with the largest x-value), and the "west" most point in the right convex hull (that is, the point with the smallest x-value), and connect them. Connect the next points in the individual convex hulls as well, to create one large cycle. This can obviously be done in $O(n)$ time. However, the resulting cycle may not be a convex polygon. We can now iterate through the cycle to eliminate the points where we have a "clock-wise" turn, also in $O(n)$ time.

Therefore, the entire merging algorithm runs in $O(n)$ time, and the entire algorithm runs in $O(n \log n)$ time.

Question 39. Overlapping Rectangles

In a 2 dimensional plane, a rectangle can be specified using the top left ("north west") and the bottom right ("south east") points. Two rectangles are said to overlap, if there is a common point that is contained in both of them. [If a rectangle is entirely contained in another, they are still said to "overlap", even though their lines don't cross.] Given n rectangles (using 2 points each), give an $O(n \log n)$ algorithm to determine if any two rectangles from the list overlap.

Solution

We divide the set of rectangles along the axis by using the median of the rectangles into three subsets: S_1, S_2 and S_3. Set S_1 consists of rectangles that lie entirely on one side of the median line, set S_2, consists of rectangles that overlap across the median, and set S_3 consists of rectangles that lie entirely on the other side of the median line. Clearly, sets S_1 and S_3 cannot overlap at all. Also, the set S_2 consists of rectangles wherein all the rectangles already overlap on one axis. To see if there is any overlapping rectangle only requires checking that the intervals overlap along the other axis. This can be done in linear time, in terms of the size of the set S_2.

However, the set S_2 needs to be considered both with the sets S_1 and S_3. This is the main complication with this divide and conquer algorithm. If the set S_2 is of small constant size, we can write the recurrence relation as:

$$T(n) = 2\, T(n/2 + c) + O(n)$$

As we know, that recurrence relation leads to a time complexity of $O(n \log n)$.

This algorithm is a fairly practical algorithm, but is not guaranteed to run in $O(n \log n)$ time as the size of the set S_2 may be large. We present an algorithm that guarantees $O(n \log n)$ time next.

Sweep line algorithm combined with an active set

The key idea is to sweep a vertical line from left to right across the plane, processing events where the vertical line intersects the left or right edges of rectangles.

For each rectangle, we generate two events: a "start" event when the sweep line encounters the left edge and an "end" event when it passes the right edge. We sort these events by the x-coordinate, ensuring that we process "start" events before "end" events if two events have the same x-coordinate.

As the sweep line moves, we maintain an active set of rectangles currently intersecting the sweep line. This active set is ordered by the y-intervals of the rectangles. When we process a "start" event, we check if the new rectangle overlaps with any existing rectangles in the active set by examining its immediate neighbors in the sorted order. If any overlap is found, we conclude that two rectangles overlap. If not, we add the rectangle to the active set. When processing an "end" event, we simply remove the corresponding rectangle from the active set. This approach ensures that we efficiently detect overlaps in *O(n log n)* time.

```python
def do_rectangles_overlap(rectangles):
  events = []

  # Create events
  for i,(x_min,y_min,x_max,y_max) in rectangles:
    events.append((x_min,      y_min,      y_max,
'start'))
    events.append((x_max, y_min, y_max, 'end'))

  # Sort events by x-coordinate
  events.sort()

  # Sweep line with active set
  active_set = SortedList()

  for event in events:
    x, y_min, y_max, event_type = event

    if event_type == 'start':
      # Check for overlap in active set
      idx = active_set.bisect((y_min, y_max))

      # Check overlap with prev/next rectangle
      if active_set[idx-1][1] > y_min:
        return true
      if active_set[idx+1][0] < y_max:
        return true

      # Add current rect. to active set
      active_set.add((y_min, y_max))

    elif event_type == 'end':
      active_set.remove((y_min, y_max))

  return false
```

Conceptual Similarity with the Closest Pair of Points Algorithm

The sweep line algorithm for detecting rectangle overlaps bears strong conceptual similarities to the *Closest Pair of Points* algorithm, particularly in its use of a dynamically updated active set. In both algorithms, a vertical sweep line is used to process a set of geometric objects (rectangles or points), maintaining an active set of objects that are currently relevant as the sweep progresses. This set is kept in sorted order, allowing for efficient checks for interactions or proximity between neighboring elements.

In the Closest Pair of Points algorithm, the goal is to find the two points that are closest to each other, which involves comparing each point with others in a narrow vertical strip as the sweep line moves. Similarly, in the rectangle overlap detection algorithm, the sweep line checks each new rectangle against neighboring rectangles in the y-sorted active set to detect overlaps. Both algorithms rely on efficient searching and sorting operations to manage the active set, enabling them to achieve a time complexity of *O(n log n)*. This shared structure underlines the versatility of the sweep line approach in solving various computational geometry problems.

Question 40. Overlapping discs

You are given *n* unit discs on the 2D plane. Each disc is specified by its center, and is a circle of radius *1*. Give an *O(n log n)* time algorithm to find if two discs overlap.

Solution

Since all discs are of radius *1*, therefore if two discs overlap, the centers of discs must be within a distance of *2*. Therefore, this question is akin to asking if the distance between the closest pair of points is less than *2* or not. For solving the closest pair of points problem, we refer the reader to the textbook (Arora, 2016), Section 4.7.

Question 41. Furthest Pair of Points

Given a set of *n* points in the *xy*-plane, design a divide and conquer algorithm that finds the **furthest** pair of points (i.e., the pair of points that are the greatest Euclidean distance apart). Your algorithm should run in *O(n log n)* time. Describe the algorithm and explain why it achieves the desired time complexity.

Solution

To find the furthest pair of points in the *xy*-plane using a divide and conquer approach, we start by computing the convex hull of the set of points. Once the convex hull is obtained, we use a simple linear scan to find the furthest pair of points.

Algorithm:

1. Compute the Convex Hull: The first step is to compute the convex hull of the set. This can be done using algorithms like Graham's scan or the divide and conquer algorithm discussed earlier, both of which run in $O(n\ log\ n)$ time. The convex hull is the smallest convex polygon that contains all the given points.

2. Finding the Furthest Pair Using Linear Search: After constructing the convex hull, the next step is to find the furthest pair of points that lie on this convex polygon.

   Key Insight: For a given edge of the convex hull, the point that is furthest from this edge must be one of the vertices of the convex hull.

   a. Start with any edge of the convex hull.

   b. Find the point that is furthest from this edge. This can be done in $O(h)$ time using a brute-force approach, where h is the number of points on the convex hull.

    c.   Move to the next edge in a clockwise order. For the next edge, the furthest point will be in the clockwise direction from previously found point.

    d.   Continue this process for all edges of the convex hull. Because each point will be considered only once as the furthest point in each iteration, the overall complexity of finding the furthest points remains $O(h)$.

3. **Calculate the Maximum Distance**: During this linear traversal, compute the Euclidean distance between the current pair of points and keep track of the maximum distance encountered.

We observe that this algorithm runs in $O(n\ log\ n)$ time, as the convex hull runs in $O(n\ log\ n)$ time and the linear scan runs in $O(n)$ time.

Note: Following questions serve as examples where a divide and conquer strategy may not be the most suitable choice. They are designed to help us identify situations where we may be tempted to use divide and conquer, but that choice is not optimal.

Question 42. Matrix Chain Multiplication, using Divide and Conquer

We are given n matrices $A_1, A, ... A_n$ of dimensions r_1 x c_1, r_2 x $c_2, ... , r_n$ x c_n, respectively. Our goal is to compute the product $A_1 A_2 ... A_n$. Specifically, **we need to determine the order in which we should multiply the matrices pairwise.** The textbook Section 6.4 presents an $O(n^3)$ dynamic programming solution for this problem. Design a divide and conquer algorithm that finds the optimal value of k — the recurrence breakpoint and analyze its time complexity.

Solution

Divide and conquer version of this algorithm really shows the inherent deficiency of this design technique, specifically with respect to overlapping subproblems.

The algorithm tries to find the best value of k by trying all possible values. Let us use $f(i,j)$ to represent the cost of multiplying matrices i through j. We can write:

$$f(1,n) = min_k \, f(1,k) + f(k+1,n) + r_i \, c_k \, c_j$$

```
// Matrix Chain Multiplication
// D&C Version (Not Optimal!)
MCMDC (p[],i, j){

  // Base Case, No Recursion
  if (i==j) {
    return 0;
  }

  // Finds the Minimum over all k
  min = Integer.MAX_VALUE;
  for (k = i;  k < j; k++) {
    c = MCMDC(p,i,k) + MCMDC(p,k+1,j) +
p[i-1]*p[k]*p[j];

    if (c < min) {
      min = c;
    }
  }
  return min;
}
```

The recurrence relation of this algorithm can be written as:

$$T(n) = 1 + \sum_{k=1 \text{ to } n-1} (T(k) + T(n-k))$$

This leads us to an exponential time complexity, that is, $T(n) = \Omega(2^n)$.

Question 43. Combination Lock and Minimum Number of Steps

You are given a circular combination lock, with the complication that the symbols on the lock can repeat. For example, the lock may have the symbols "a, b, a, c, d, b, a, d" arranged in a usual circular pattern. Further, you are given a code, which may have repetitions as well. You are required to construct the shortest path to generate that code. For example, given the lock *[a, b, a, c, d, c, b, a, d]*, and the code *[c, c, b]* we can generate the code in a total of *3 (clockwise) + 0 (no move) + 2 (counterclockwise) = 5* steps, where a step is defined as rotating the lock one position in either clockwise or anti-clockwise direction. The first element in the array is the symbol at which the lock is currently pointing.

Given an array of size n that represents the lock, and an array of size m that represents the target code, give a divide and conquer algorithm to calculate the shortest distance for the code.

We can assume that every symbol in the code is present in the lock as well, so it is feasible to generate the code.

Solution

For a recursive formulation, we can use the following notation:

$f(S,C)$ represents the cost of generating the code C, from the Lock Array S

Suppose the first element of the code array c_1 exists k times in the Lock Array S at locations: s_{11}, s_{12}, ..., s_{1k}. An exhaustive search can generate the first code symbol with any of the lock array symbols. Thus, we can write the recurrence relation as:

$$f(S,C) = min\{1 \leq i \leq k\}\ \{d_i + f(S(i),\ C - c_1)\}$$

Here, d_i represents the cost of rotating the lock to s_{1i} which is the cost of the minimum of the clockwise and counterclockwise direction moves, and $S(i)$ represents the new lock array S, that is now rotated to the s_{1i}. $C - c_1$ is part of the code that still needs to be generated after the first letter c_1 has been generated.

The time complexity recurrence relation can be written in terms of the length of the code that needs to be generated, and using the observation that $k \leq n$:

$$T(m) = n\ T(m-1)$$

Thus, the overall time complexity of the algorithm is $O(n^m)$. Obviously, this time complexity is exponential, and therefore, not very good.   There are other algorithm design techniques that can solve this problem in more efficient manner.

Section 4: Greedy Algorithms

Question 44. Interval scheduling

Suppose you are given a list of lectures with their start time and end times. How can you choose the maximum number of non-overlapping lectures?

This problem is also sometimes articulated as the party planning problem:

*You are asked to be the organizer for n parties and are provided with their start and end times. (For example: P1: 7 AM – 9 AM; P2: 8 AM to 3 PM; P3: 4 AM to 8 AM.) You can only be organizing one party at a time, so you need to choose. For every party that you organize, you are given a fixed reward (1000$) irrespective of the length of the party. How do you select the parties to **maximize your reward**? What is the time complexity of your algorithm in terms of n?*

Solution

Suppose the list of lectures are given by their start and end times as:

$[[s_1, e_1], [s_2, e_2], ... [s_n, e_n]]$

Firstly, we prove that the following greedy choice property holds: there is an optimal schedule with non-overlapping lectures that includes the first ending lecture.

Theorem: There is an optimal schedule with non-overlapping lectures that includes the first ending lecture.

Proof (By Contradiction): For the purpose of contraction, we assume that there is no optimal schedule with non-overlapping lectures that includes the first ending lecture.

Without loss of generality, suppose an optimal schedule is given as S. We construct a schedule S' as follows:

We remove the very first ending lecture in S and add the first ending lecture overall, which consists of interval $[s_1, e_1]$.

We observe that S' is a feasible schedule. Further S' schedules as many lectures as the given optimal schedule S. Further S' includes the first ending lecture. This contradicts the assumption that there is no optimal schedule with non-overlapping lectures that includes the first ending lecture.

Having established the greedy choice property, we can simply sort the lectures by their end time and iterate the lectures

```
Step 1: Sort the lectures by increasing end
times
// O(n log n) time

Step 2: Initialize ending time of selected
lectures to negative infinity
// O(1) time

Step 3: For j = 1 to n
     If j-th lecture starts after the
ending time, then:
          Select j-th lecture and update
ending time
Otherwise, skip.
// O(n) time
```

The overall algorithm runs in *O(n log n)* time.

Question 45. Maximum Spanning Tree

Consider problem similar to a minimum spanning tree, but instead we want to find the maximum spanning tree, that is, a tree that maximums the sum of weights of the edges. Describe an efficient algorithm to find the maximum spanning tree.

Solution

The greedy choice property still holds. We can replace each edge cost with the corresponding negative value, or simply change the ordering in the algorithm as follows:

```
// Given a graph and its weight matrix
// Find a maximum spanning tree
Algorithm MaxST (in:G, W[1:n,1:n]; out:T)
Sort edges in descending order of weight:
e[1], e[2], .. e[m].
Initialize counter j = 1
Initialize tree T to empty
While (number of edges in Tree < n-1) {
   If adding the edge e[j] does not create a
cycle,
      add edge e[j] to tree T
   Increment j
}
```

Question 46. Maximum Product Spanning Tree

Consider problem similar to a minimum or maximum spanning tree, but instead we want to find the maximum product spanning tree, that is, a tree that maximums the product of weights of the edges. Describe an efficient algorithm to find the maximum product spanning tree. Assume that weight of each edge is at least *1*.

Solution

We note that the sum of log values is equal to the sum of product values. Therefore, this problem can be reduced to the maximum spanning tree problem by replacing each edge weight with its log value.

Question 47. Optimal Symbol Encoding

Given a set of symbols and their frequency of usage, find a binary code for each symbol, such that:

a. Binary code for any symbol is not the prefix of the binary code of another symbol.

b. The weighted length of codes for all the symbols (weighted by the usage frequency) is minimized.

Solution

This is the Huffman encoding problem. The intuition behind the algorithm is that more frequent symbols should have shorter codes, and less frequent symbols should have longer codes. This can be implemented using an approach where we take the two least frequent symbols and combine them into a virtual symbol that appears with a frequency that is equal to the sum of the individual frequencies of the two symbols.

This can be implemented using the following greedy algorithm that utilizes a minimum heap.

1. Initialize an empty encoding tree.
2. Create a min-heap of all the symbols in the alphabet based on the frequency.
3. While there are more than two symbols in the alphabet:
   a. Extract the two symbols with least frequencies by invoking the extract minimum operation two times.
   b. Create a node with the sum of two frequencies and insert it back into the heap. Also insert this node in the encoding tree with the two symbols as its left and right child nodes.
4. When only two symbols are left, create a root node for the encoding tree and the two symbols become the child nodes of the root node.

This algorithm results in a binary tree in which the symbols end up as leaves, with the lowest frequency nodes farthest away from the root and highest frequency nodes in leaves closer to the top. From the root, assign 0 and 1 to the edges from each parent node. The code for a symbol will be the concatenation of the edges on its path. The depth for any particular character is the length of the path, which is also be the length for the code word for that character.

We observe that there may be more than one Huffman code; no code is uniquely optimal. The set of lengths of an optimal code might not be unique. However, the expected value or the weighted average $\sum(i=1)^n$ {frequency[i]*code_length[i])} will be the same and will be minimized.

Question 48. Unit Intervals on Number Line

Given a set $\{x_1, x_2, x_3, ... x_n\}$ of points on the real line, determine the smallest set of unit-length closed intervals (e.g., the interval [1.25,2.25] includes all x_i such that $1.25 \leq x_i \leq 2.25$ that contains all of the points. Give the most efficient algorithm you can to solve this problem, prove it is correct and analyze the time complexity.

Solution

The idea of this algorithm is very similar to the interval scheduling problem above. We can prove that the following greedy algorithm is optimal:

1. Order all the points $\{x_1, x_2, x_3, ... x_n\}$
2. Make the first unit interval that starts at x_1

3. Eliminate all points that are contained in that unit interval
4. Continue until all points are covered.

Question 49. Fast Response Server Placement

A series of client machines *[1, 2, ... n]* are located along a linear network. The *i*-th client generates amount of traffic that is given by *w[i]*. You want to put a server somewhere along the linear network that minimizes the total amount of traffic carried by the network. Total traffic is given by sum of each client's individual traffic, multiplied by the distance (the number of hops) from the server. Provide an *O(n)* algorithm to identify the location of the server.

Solution

We observe that the greedy choice of placing the server at the median (by weight) location minimizes the cost. Optimality can be proved using a proof by contradiction.

Based on this observation, a simple algorithm can be written as follows:

1. Iterate the weight array from left to right and find out the TOTAL weight. This step takes O(n) time

2. Iterate the weight array again from right to left and find the point at which the accumulated weight meets or exceeds half of total weight. We place the proxy server on that location.

Examples: As with any other problem, using a few examples often helps to improve our understanding of the solution.

- Given [1, 1, 1, 1], we put the proxy server on the 2nd location (or the 3rd location)
- Given [1, 1, 1, 1, 1], we put the proxy server on the 3rd location
- Given [1,2,3,4], put the proxy server on the 3rd location.
- Given [1,2,3,10], put the proxy server on the 4th location.
- Given [10,1,1,1,1,1,1], put the proxy server on the 1st location.

Question 50. Greedy Vertex Coloring Algorithm

The chromatic number of G is denoted as $\chi(G)$ and is defined as the smallest number of colors needed to color the graph so that no two adjacent nodes receive the same color.

Using a greedy coloring algorithm prove that the $\chi(G) \leq \Delta(G)+1$, where $\Delta(G)$ is the largest degree in the graph.

Solution

Let the vertices of a graph G be $v_1, v_2, ..., v_n$ and the maximum degree of G be Δ. For $i = 1, 2, ..., n$ we color v_i with the smallest number that is available, i.e., the number that has not been used on the vertices in $\{v_1, v_2, ..., v_{i-1}\}$ that are adjacent to v_i. Since there are at most Δ vertices that are adjacent to v_i, this algorithm will not use more than $\Delta + 1$ colors. Therefore, we have $\chi(G) \leq \Delta(G)+1$.

Question 51. Cover Negatives with Positives

You are given an integer k, and an array of n elements, where each element is either P (for positive), or N (for negative). You want to match each N, with a P, such that: (i) each positive can only cover one negative, and (ii) a positive can cover a negative only if it is within k distance. We want to maximize the negatives that are covered. For example, given the following array: [P, P, P, N, N] and $k=1$, we can only cover one N, using the assignment (3->4). However, given the same array and $k=2$, we can cover both Ns using assignment (2->4, 3->5).

Give an efficient polynomial-time algorithm to maximize the Ns that are covered.

Solution

The greedy choice property here is that a positive number tries to cover the leftmost uncovered negative number that is within the k distance. To implement this greedy choice property, we use the following algorithm:

We maintain two array pointers x and y, x for positive numbers and y for negative numbers. Both pointers start from the left end, so they are initialized to the index of the first positive number and the first negative number respectively. If $|x-y| \leq k$, then we cover the positive number $a[x]$ with the negative number $a[y]$, and increment both the x and y pointers to next positive and negative numbers respectively. If $|x-y| > k$, we simply increment the smaller of the two indices x and y.

As we observe from the algorithm, in each time unit, we increment at least one of x or y. Further, both x and y start from the left end of the array and the values are never decremented. Therefore, this algorithm runs in $O(n)$ time.

Question 52. Stack of Coins

You are given n stacks of coins. The i-th stack has s_i coins of value v_i each. In this turn-based game, the objective is to collect the maximum value by selecting the top of any (non-empty) stack and realizing the value of that coin. Once the coin is selected, it is removed from the stack and plays no further role in the game. Give an efficient polynomial time algorithm to determine the maximum total value we can realize if we move first. We can assume that the opponent uses the same optimal strategy.

Solution

We observe that a simple greedy algorithm can solve this problem. While there are versions of this problem that require dynamic programming, in this specific version, simply ordering the stacks in order of the coins from the highest to the lowest is sufficient.

Algorithm:

1. Initialize the total value collected as total_value = 0.
2. While there are still coins remaining in any stack:
   a. Identify the stack that has the top coin with the maximum value. If there are multiple stacks with the same top value, select any of them.

b. Add the value of the top coin from the selected stack to your total value if it's your turn, otherwise, let the opponent take it (this turn doesn't count towards your total value).

c. Remove the coin from the selected stack.

3. Continue alternating turns between you and the opponent until all stacks are empty.

Section 5:   Dynamic Programming

Question 53. Matrix Chain Multiplication – Non-Dynamic Programming Variations

The context of this question is the matrix chain multiplication problem, for which there is an $O(n^3)$ dynamic programming solution. In this question, we consider two non-dynamic programming variations.

Variation 1: Divide and Conquer Algorithm

In the context of matrix chain multiplication problem, consider a divide and conquer algorithm that finds the optimal value of "k" by defining the same recurrence relation as used in the dynamic programming algorithm. Find the time complexity of such a divide and conquer algorithm.

Solution

We use the notation where $M(1,n)$ represents the minimum cost to multiply the sequence of matrices from 1 to n.

The recursive formulation is written as:

$$M(1,n) = min_k \{M(1,k) + r[i]*c[k]*c[j] + M(k+1,n)\}$$

Time complexity of this can be written as:

$$T(n) = \sum_{k=1 \; to \; n} \{T(k) + T(n-k-1) + O(1)\}$$

This can be simplified to:

$$T(n) = O(n) + 2 \sum_{k=1 \; to \; (n-1)} \{T(k)\}$$

This clearly leads to an exponential time. Considering that the dynamic programming formulation runs in $O(n^3)$ time, the dynamic programming formulation is highly favored over this particular divide and conquer formulation.

Variation 2: Greedy Algorithm

In the context of matrix chain multiplication problem, consider a greedy algorithm that simply chooses to first multiply two matrices that minimize the cost of that multiplication operation. **Give a specific example sequence of matrix dimensions** in which the greedy algorithm does not minimize the overall cost of matrix chain multiplication.

Solution

Consider the following sequence of 3 matrices:

(20 x 2) (2 x 10) (10 x 30)

In this sequence, we observe that the greedy algorithm chooses to multiple first two matrices first, since the cost of that operation is *400*, compared to *600* to that of the alternative. In this case, the total computation cost becomes: *400 + 6000*, that is, *6400*.

The optimal sequence is to multiply the right two matrices first, and in that case, the cost is *600 + 1200*, that is, *1800*, which is approximately a third of that of the greedy algorithm cost.

So, we observe that the greedy algorithm that chooses to first multiply two matrices that minimize the cost of that multiplication operation is not optimal.

Question 54. Shining: Barbie's Array of Diamonds

Barbie has *n* diamonds. Each diamond has two attributes: shiny value and weight value. Barbie wants to create a "diamond line" in which each diamond is both shinier and heavier than the previous one. She may not be able to use all her diamonds, but wants to maximize the number of diamonds in this diamond line. Give a polynomial time algorithm for creating a diamond line with maximum number of diamonds. Assume that her initial list of diamonds is not in any specific order.

Solution

This question can be solved as an application of the Longest Increasing Subsequence (LIS) problem, by first sorting the given list of diamonds along one attribute, and using the second attribute in LIS.

The overall time complexity is $O(n^2)$ and can be reduced to $O(n \log n)$ by using binary search in the second step.

Question 55. Love (Skip) Thy Neighbor

Given a list of *n* positive numbers, your objective is to select the set of numbers that maximizes the sum of selected numbers, given the constraint that we cannot select two numbers that are located adjacent to each other. Describe a **linear time algorithm** for this problem.

Solution

Suppose the given array is *a*, with values *a[1], .., a[n]*. Let *S(j)* denote the maximum sum of numbers that can be achieved using first *j* numbers, such that no adjacent numbers are selected.

We observe that *S(j)* can be defined recursively as follows:

$$S(j) = max \{S(j-1), S(j-2) + a[j]\}$$

The two arguments in the *max* function correspond to the cases where we select *(j − 1)*-th element and forego *j*-th element, or we select *j*-th element and forego *(j − 1)*-th element.

This recursive relationship can be seeded with the following two base values:

$$S(1) = a[1]$$

$$S(2) = max\{a[1], a[2]\}$$

We observe that the principle of optimality clearly holds in this case, as if *S(j)* is optimal, then the sub-solutions *S(j-1)* and *S(j-2)* must be optimal as well.

Therefore, the following dynamic programming algorithm can be used.

```
S[1] = a[1]
S[2] = max{a[1], a[2]}
for j = 3 to n
    S[j] = max {S[j-1], S[j-2]+a[j]

// Our final answer is S[n]
```

Due to the simple one loop in the algorithm, the time complexity is *O(n)*.

As with other dynamic programming algorithms, we observe that while there is a recursive relationship, the algorithm itself has no recursive calls.

Question 56. Around the block party planning

Consider a row of *n* houses represented as an array: *A[1..n]*, where the phrase "next door neighbor" having its natural meaning. Each resident is assigned a "fun factor" *F[1..n]*, which represents how much fun they bring to a party. Your goal is to maximize the fun of a party that you are arranging, but with the constraint that you cannot select three consecutive neighbors. (So for example, if you invite the *A[5]* and *A[6]* family, you cannot invite the *A[4]* or *A[7]* families.) Give an efficient algorithm to select the guest list.

Solution

Let *S(j)* denote the maximum fun factor that can be achieved using first *j* numbers, such that no consecutive three numbers are selected.

We observe that *S(j)* can be defined recursively as follows:

$$S(j) = max \{S(j-1), S(j-2)+a[j], S(j-3)+a[j-1]+a[j]\}$$

The arguments in the *max* function correspond to the 3 cases about which number is not included in the selection.

This recursive relationship can be seeded with the following base values:

$S(1) = a[1]$

$S(2) = a[1] + a[2]$

$S(3) = max \{a[1]+a[3], a[2]+a[3], a[1]+a[2]\}$

We observe that the principle of optimality clearly holds in this case. If we are able to find a better value for sub-solutions, then we will be able to find a better value for solution as well.

Therefore, ▪ the following dynamic programming algorithm can be used.

```
S[1] = a[1]
S[2] = a[1] + a[2]
S[4] = max{S[2], a[1] + a[3], a[2] + a[3]}
for j = 4 to n
    S[j] = max {S[j-1], S[j-2]+a[j], S[j-3]+a[j-1]+a[j]}

// Our final answer is S[n]
```

Due to the simple one loop in the algorithm, the time complexity is $O(n)$.

As with other dynamic programming algorithms, we observe that while there is a recursive relationship, the algorithm itself has no recursive calls.

Question 57. Longest Path in a Directed Acyclic Graph

You are given a Directed Acyclic Graph (DAG) with n vertices and m edges. The weight of edge (u, v) in the graph is given by $w(u,v)$. Write an algorithm to find the weight of the maximum weight path in the graph.

Solution

To find the longest path in a DAG, dynamic programming combined with topological sorting is an effective approach. The basic idea is to process the vertices in a topological order and update the longest path for each vertex.

Steps:

1. Topological Sort: Perform a topological sort on the DAG. This ordering ensures that for every directed edge (u, v), vertex u comes before v in the order. Topological sort takes $O(n+m)$ time.

2. Initialize Distances: Create a distance array $d[]$, where $d[i]$ represents the longest distance to vertex i from any starting vertex. Initialize $d[i] = -\infty$ for all i, except the starting vertices which are initialized to 0.

3. Dynamic Programming: Traverse each vertex u in topological order. For each

vertex u, update its neighboring vertices v with $d[v] = max(d[v], d[u] + weight(u, v))$.

4. Result: The length of the longest path in the DAG is the maximum value in the $d[]$ array after all vertices have been processed.

The total time complexity is $O(n+m)$.

Question 58. Maximum Value Contiguous Problem Variations

In the context of Maximum Value Contiguous problem, (i) What can be a greedy algorithm? (ii) What can be a Divide and Conquer algorithm?

Solution

A greedy algorithm can be created that simply selects the maximum element first, and then iterates both forward and backward such that the overall sum is maximized. This algorithm also runs in $O(n)$ time, but may not give optimal result, as the maximum element may not be a part of the optimal sequence.

A divide and conquer algorithm for the MVCS problem can work as follows:

Consider any element of the array, $a[j]$ to be a point in the maximum value contiguous subsequence. We can find the optimal sequence by traversing the parts of the array to the left and to the right of j in $O(n)$ time. Therefore, for all n possible values of j, the algorithm runs in $O(n^2)$ time. Due to its exhaustive nature, it always finds the optimal result, but its time complexity is larger than that of the $O(n)$ dynamic programming algorithm.

Question 59. Canoeing on the cheap

You are canoeing down a river and there are n renting posts along the way. Before starting your journey, you are given, for each $1 \leq i \leq j \leq n$, the fee $f(i,j)$ for renting a canoe from post i to post j. These fees are arbitrary. For example it is possible that $f(1,3)= 10$ and $f(1,4) = 5$. You begin at trading post 1 and must end at trading post n (using rented canoes). Your goal is to minimize the rental cost. Give the most efficient algorithm you can for this problem. Prove that your algorithm yields an optimal solution and analyze the time complexity.

Solution

Since we start from the trading post 1, we can use a simple, one dimensional notation.

Notation

Suppose $g(j)$ represents the minimum cost of reaching the j-th post (starting from trading post 1).

Base Case

As an initial value, we set $g(1) = 0$.

Recursive Formulation

$$g(j) = min_{1 \leq i < j} \{g(i) + f(i,j)\}$$

Optimality

We can prove that $g(j)$ is the optimal value using a proof by induction on j. The base case holds easily as $g(1) = 0$. Suppose $g(j)$ is optimal for all values of $j < m$. Then, let us consider $g(m)$. Suppose, for the purpose of contradiction that $g(m)$ is not optimal, and that there exists a path with smaller cost to reach the j-th post. Then, there are two cases. Either that shortest path is a straight edge from the post 1 to the post j, or it is not. The first case is easily ruled out, as $g(j)$ has $f(1,j)$ as one of the terms in its minimum clause. Similarly, the second case is ruled out as $g(j)$ is optimal for all values of $j < m$. Therefore, $g(m)$ must also be optimal, and by principle of mathematical induction, $g(j)$ is optimal for all values of j.

Algorithm

Like many other dynamic programming algorithms, once the recurrence relation is finalized, the algorithm itself is obvious. For this problem, we can write it as follows:

```
for j = 2 to n
    g[j] = min (g[i] + f[i][j])
    // Over all values of 1 ≤ i < j
```

From the algorithm, it is clear that the time complexity is $O(n^2)$, as there are n values to calculate, and it takes $O(n)$ time to calculate each value.

Therefore, the overall time complexity of this algorithm is $O(n^2)$.

Question 60. A Profitable TV Network (!)

A TV network has n minutes of advertising time to sell during a prime-time show. The network can sell the time in various slot lengths, with each slot length having a corresponding price that advertisers are willing to pay. Given n (total advertising time), a list *lengths* of possible slot lengths, and a list *prices* of what advertisers pay for each slot, determine the maximum revenue the network can make by selling the n minutes. For example, with $n = 10$, *lengths* = [3, 5, 7], and *prices* = [8, 15, 20], the maximum revenue is 30 dollars by selling two 5-minute slots. Use dynamic programming to find the optimal slot combination for maximum revenue.

Solution

As suggested, we use the concept of Dynamic Programming and follow the usual NORA approach.

Notation

Let $dp[i]$ represent the maximum revenue that can be obtained by selling i minutes of advertising time. We observe that we are really interested in finding $dp[n]$.

Optimality

The goal is to find the maximum revenue for exactly n minutes of advertising time by optimally selecting from the available slot lengths. For each minute i (from 0 to n), we need to consider every possible slot length that can fit into i and maximize the revenue by considering all possible combinations.

Recurrence Relation

The maximum revenue $dp[i]$ for i minutes can be derived using the following relation:

$$dp[i] = max_j \{dp[i], dp[i - lengths[j]] + prices[j]\}$$

Here, j ranges over all slot lengths such that $lengths[j] \leq i$. This means that for each minute i, we check every possible slot length $lengths[j]$ that can fit into i and update $dp[i]$ by considering the revenue from that slot plus the maximum revenue obtainable for the remaining time *i - lengths[j]*.

Algorithm

1. Initialize: Create an array *dp* of size *n+1*, where *dp[0] = 0* (no revenue for *0* minutes) and initialize all other elements to *0*.
2. Iterate over total time:

```
// Representing each minute from 1 to n):
for i = 1 to n
  for each j where lengths[j] ≤ i:
    // update dp[i] as follows:
    dp[i] = max j { dp[i], dp[i -
lengths[j]] + prices[j]}
```

Question 61. Magical eggs and tiny floors[1]

You are given *m* eggs and a *n* floor building. You need to figure out the highest floor an egg can be dropped without breaking, assuming that (i) all eggs are identical, (ii) if an egg breaks after being dropped

---

[1] This problem is found on many internet forums, and was apparently also used in a Google job interview. The problem can also be posed in the form of cell phone drop testing, by replacing eggs with cell phones, etc.

from one floor, then the egg will also break if dropped from all higher floors, and (iii) if an egg does not break after being thrown from a certain floor, it retains all of its strength and you can continue to use that egg. Your goal is to minimize the number of throws. From which floor do you drop the first egg?

Solution

We begin by making an observation about the base case. Suppose we only have access to one egg, that is, $m = 1$. Then, we are forced to try each floor one by one, starting with the lowest floor.

Secondly, we note the asymmetry in this problem by observing that given two eggs, if we use the default "binary search" idea and drop the first egg from the 50th floor, that is not necessarily optimal since if the egg breaks, then we are left with only one egg for the lower 50 floors, while if the egg doesn't break, we are left with two eggs for the upper 50 floors. Hence, there is some difference in the amount of "resources" (eggs, in this case) between the two cases.

Based on these two observations, we can write the recursive formulation as follows:

Notation

Let $f(n,m)$ be the minimum number of attempts given n floors and m eggs.

Base Cases

$f(n,1) = n$ // We have no option but to climb floors one by one.

Similarly, $f(1,m) = 1$ // We just need one try if there is only one floor

Recursive Formulation

The recursion is built around the first action – which floor do we try the first egg from. Suppose the first egg is thrown from the j-th floor. Then, if the egg breaks, then we have $j-1$ floors left, $m-1$ eggs left. If the egg doesn't break, then we have $n-j$ floors and m eggs left. We want to minimize our worst-case scenario. That is, we want to minimize the maximum of those two scenarios.

Thus, the recursion we get is:

$$f(n,m) = \min_{1 \leq j \leq n} \{\max \{f(j-1,m-1), f(n-j,m)\} + 1\}$$

Algorithm

This leads to a straightforward dynamic programming formulation, which has mn entries in the dynamic programming table and each entry can be computed in at most n time, Therefore, the algorithm runs in $O(n^2 m)$ time.

Improved Algorithm

The time complexity can be improved to $O(n\,m)$ by observing that optimal first attempt floor for $(n,m) \geq$ optimal first attempt floor for $(n-1,m)$. So, when executing the loop on n, we don't need to start the j counter with an initial value of 1. Therefore, we can compute all $f(n,m)$ values for one value of m and all values of n in $O(n)$ time.

Question 62. Teleportation

You have a teleporter that can take you from galaxy i to galaxy j. Cost to teleport is given by $c(i,j) > 0$, which can be arbitrary. Some galaxies are "astro-haunted" - this is specified by a matrix A, where $A[i]$ can be 0 or 1 (1 means that that galaxy is "astro-haunted"). Give a polynomial time algorithm that minimizes the cost of going from galaxy 1 to galaxy n, such that you pass through at most m astro-haunted galaxies. (You can assume that galaxies 1 and n are not astro-haunted.)

Solution

We observe that the problem is similar to all pairs shortest path problem, but in addition to that, we have the constraint that we can go through at most m astro-haunted galaxies. We model this constraint also in our notation.

Notation

Let $D(i,j,k)$ denote the cost of the shortest path from i to j using at most k astro-haunted galaxies.

Recursive Formulation

Recursive formulation on $D(i,j,k)$ can be written on the variable k and by deciding on the last astro-haunted galaxy on the path from i to j.

$$D(i,j,k) = min \{$$
$$D(i,j,k-1),$$
$$min_{(1 \leq z \leq n \mid A[z]=1)} \{D(i,z,k-1) + D(z,j,0)\}$$
$$\}$$

We observe that $A[z] = 1$ constraint specifies that the galaxy z is astro haunted.

Further, by taking the minimum with $D(i,j,k-1)$ we satisfy the constraint of *at most k* astro-haunted galaxies, while still avoiding pitfall of leaving this value undefined in case there is no astro haunted galaxy.

Base Case

Base case $D(i,j,0)$ can be solved simply by using All Pairs Shortest Path and by eliminating all astro-haunted galaxies.

Algorithm

The algorithm can easily be written in terms of for loops for each of the indices in the notation of $D(i,j,k)$. As is often observed, the index of the main recursive formulation usually forms the outermost loop.

```
// Step 1: Base Case
Calculate D[i][j][0] as All Pairs Shortest
path by ignoring the astro haunted
galaxies.

// Step 2: Inductive Step
for k = 1 to m
  for i = 1 to n
    for j = 1 to n
      Calculate       D[i][j][k]      =      min
{D([i][j][k-1], D[i][z][k-1] + D[z][j][0]
for all z such that A[z] = 1}
```

Time Complexity

Time Complexity of base case: $O(n^3)$ from the all pairs shortest path problem. Each calculation of $D(i,j,k)$ takes $O(n)$ time. Further, there are kn^2 entries in the dynamic programming table. Therefore, the total time Complexity of recursive portion: $O(k\,n^3)$

Therefore, the total time complexity is $O(k\,n^3)$.

Question 63. Longest Common Subsequence

Given two strings (sequences of characters), the longest common subsequence (LCS) problem is to find the longest subsequence (not necessarily contiguous) that exists in both of the input strings. For example, given strings "mangoes" and "mementos", the subsequence "mnos" is common in both and is in fact the longest common subsequence. Given two strings of sizes n_1 and n_2 respectively, find a dynamic programming algorithm to find the longest common subsequence in $O(n_1 n_2)$ time.

Solution

Before we formalize a dynamic programming solution for this problem, we can explore the recursive nature of this problem.

Given two strings s_1 and s_2, if the first character of both the strings is the same, then we can consider that common character to be the start of the common subsequence, and recursively call the function on the substrings of s_1 and s_2 after removing the first character. If, on the other hand, the first character is not the same, then we can discard the first character from one of the strings and evaluate the longest common subsequence with the other string. This underlying recursive idea can now be used to formulate a dynamic programming solution.

Notation

Let *LCS[i,j]* represent the length of the longest common subsequence for string s_1 starting from it's *i-*

th character and string s_2 starting from it's j-th character. We assume the strings to be 0-indexed, that is, the first character is at 0-th index.

We are interested in $LCS[0,0]$ as our final answer.

Recursive Formulation

The recursive formulation depends upon whether or not $s_1[i] = s_2[j]$.

If $s_1[i] = s_2[j]$:

$$LCS[i,j] = 1 + LCS[i+1, j+1]$$

On the other hand, if $s_1[i] \mathrel{!=} s_2[j]$:

$$LCS[i,j] = max\{LCS[i,j+1], LCS[i+1,j]\}$$

The base cases of this recursive formulation can be:

$$LCS[n_1 - 1, j] = 0 \quad \forall j$$

$$LCS[i, n_2 - 1] = 0 \quad \forall i$$

Algorithm

Since the optimal substructure property is clear from the recursive formulation of the solution, the main decision in the algorithm is in deciding the sequence in which to calculate the values. That decision is primarily driven by the order in which the values become available. For example, to compute $LCS[0,0]$, we would need values such as $LCS[1,1]$ which we would not have. Therefore, the correct sequence is to start with larger values of *i* and *j*.

```
// 2-dim int array, initialized to 0
// Length of the longest common subsequence
int[][] lcs = new int[n₁][n₂]

// 2-dim character array to store first
//   common  character  of  longest  common
subsequence
// Initialize to a character that is outside
// the characters in s1 and s2 to denote null
char[][] fcs = new char[n₁][n₂]

// Base case
for j = n₂ - 1 down to 0
lcs[n₁-1][j] = 0

for i = n₁ - 1 down to 0
     lcs[i][n₂-1] = 0

for i = n₁ - 2 down to 0
  for j = n₂ - 2 down to 0
    if s1[i] == s2[j] then
      lcs[i][j] = 1 + lcs[i+1][j+1]
      fcs[i][j] = s1[i]  // same as s2[j]
    else
      lcs[i][j] = max{lcs[i+1][j],lcs[i][j+1]}
      fcs[i][j] = fcs[i+1][j] or fcs[i][j+1]
    // depending on which lcs value was larger
    end if
```

We observe that this algorithm uses $O(n_1 n_2)$ space and takes $O(n_1 n_2)$ time.

Question 64. Maximum Value but Limited Neighbors

You are given an array *a[1..n]* of positive numbers and an integer *k*. You have to produce an array *b[1..n]*, such that: (i) For each *j*, *b[j]* is *0* or *1*, (ii) Array *b* has adjacent *1s* at most *k* times, and (iii) $\sum_{j=1\ to\ n}$ (a[j]*b[j]) is maximized. For example, given an array *[100, 300, 400, 50]* and integer *k = 1*, the array *b* can be: *[0 1 1 0]*, which maximizes the sum to be *700*. Or, given an array *[10, 100, 300, 400, 50, 4500, 200, 30, 90]* and *k = 2*, the array *b* can be *[1, 0, 1, 1, 0, 1, 1, 0, 1]* which maximizes the sum to *5500*.

Solution

We observe that this problem has obvious similarities with the "Love (Skip) Thy Neighbor" problem described above. In that problem we are not allowed to select any neighbors at all, while here, we can break that rule a total of up to *k* times.

For this problem we focus on the notation and the recursive formulation. The algorithm can then be created from the recursive formulation using loops in an intuitive manner.

Notation

Let us use *MVBLN(i, m)* to denote the sum of maximum value but limited neighbors for the array *a[1..i]* such that it includes neighbors at most *m* times.

Recursive Formulation

Recursive nature of the MVBLN problem can be formulated by observing that at the *i*-th element, we either skip the *i*-th element altogether, or we include it as a neighbor, or we include it as a non-neighbor.

$$MVBLN(i,m) = max \{MVBLN(i-1,m), MVBLN(i-1,m-1) + a[i], MVBLN(i-2,m) + a[i]\}$$

The base case of this recursive formulation is *MVBLN(i,0)* which can be computed using the "Love (Skip) Thy Neighbor" solution presented before.

The algorithm itself consists of two loops: the outer loop on the second index *m* (going from *1* to *k*, and the inner loop on the index *i*, going from *1* to *n*.

Question 65. If you are happy and you know it, jump up high!

You are standing on step 0 of a staircase. Your goal is to reach the step *n*. At each step *i*, you have three choices hop to next step *i+1*, *i+2* or *i+3*. Give an algorithm to count the number of possible paths to reach *n*.

Solution

The recursive formulation of this problem is rather straight forward. Let us denote number of possible paths starting from the step i. as $S(i)$. Then, we can write $S(i)$ as:

$$S(i) = S(i+1) + S(i+2) + S(i+3) \qquad \forall i \leq n\text{-}3$$

As a base case, we can write that:

$$S(n) = 0$$

$$S(n\text{-}1) = 1$$

$$S(n\text{-}2) = 2$$

This recursive formulation lends itself to a simple $O(n)$ algorithm to compute $S(0)$, which represents the number of possible paths to reach step n starting from step 0.

Question 66. Fast Response k-Server Placement

A series of client machines $[1, 2, \dots n]$ are located along a linear network. The i-th client generates amount of traffic that is given by $w[i]$. You want to place k servers along the linear network that minimizes the total amount of traffic carried by the network. Total traffic is given by sum of each client's individual traffic, multiplied by the distance (the number of hops) from the server. Provide a polynomial time algorithm to identify the optimal locations for *k* servers.

Solution

This problem is similar to many other placement problems. However, in this problem, the network given is all in one line (linear network), and the distance specified is in number of hops. These are significant simplifications to the problem, and the resulting algorithm is relatively simple as well. If on the other hand the network is a general graph, the problem can easily become NP-complete.

One observation to make in this problem is that if there is only one server, i.e., *k=1*, then the problem reduces to the "Fast Response Server Placement" problem for which we presented a greedy algorithm that runs in $O(n)$ time. Therefore, the base case for this problem is readily available.

Notation

Let *w(i,j,m)* denote the optimal weight using *{i..j}* client machines and *m* servers.

Recursive Formulation

w(i,j,m) can then be written as follows.

$$w(i,j,m) = min \{w(i,x,m-1) + w(x+1,j,1)\} \quad \forall x \{i \leq x \leq j-1\}$$

We observe that this algorithm uses $O(n^2k)$ space as there are n^2k entries in the dynamic programming table for the variable w. Further, we require $O(n)$ time to compute each entry. Therefore, the algorithm as formulated above takes $O(n^3k)$ time. This time complexity can be reduced to $O(n^2k)$ time by observing that the "breakpoint" (that is, the point that minimizes weighted cost) for clients $i..j+1$ can only be after the break point for clients $i..j$. Therefore, in the loop to compute $w(i,j,m)$, we do not need to start the break point search from 1, rather breakpoint for all n values of j can be found in $O(n)$ time.

Question 67. Optimal Coin Game

You are given an array of n coins of values $[v_1, v_2, ... v_n]$. In this turn-based game, the objective is to collect the maximum value by selecting either the very first or the very last coin from the array and realizing the value of that coin. Once the coin is selected, it is removed from the array and plays no further role in the game. Give an efficient polynomial time algorithm to determine the maximum total value we can realize if we move first. We can assume that the opponent uses the same optimal strategy.

Solution

As always, we begin with an intuitive notation for this problem.

Notation

Let $MCV(V, i, j)$ denote the maximum coin value that we can obtain given the list of coins $V[i..j]$. Further, let $S(V,i,j)$ denote the sum of the values of all the coins in $V[i..j]$.

Recursive Formulation

We observe that once the first player pockets the first or the last coin, the opponent realizes the maximum value from the remaining list. Therefore, the value realized by the first player is the sum of the list minus the value realized by the opponent. Therefore, we can write $MCV(V,i,j)$ as:

$$MCV(V,i,j) = \max\{S(V,i,j) - MCV(V - v_i), S(V,i,j) - MCV(V - v_j)\}$$

This can further be written as:

$$MCV(V,i,j) = S(V,i,j) - \min\{MCV(V - v_i), MCV(V - v_j)\}$$

The base case of the recurrence can be set as $MCV(\varphi) = 0$, or equivalently that the value that can be realized by a single element list is the value of that element.

Algorithm

This algorithm works like many other algorithms that need to "grow" the range of the array. Specifically, the iterations can work as follows:

```
double[][] S = new double[n][n];
double[][] MCV = new double[n][n];

// Initialize S[i,i] = V[i]
// Initialize MCV[i,i] = V[i]

for i = 0 to n-2
  for j = i+1 to n-1
    S[i,j] = S[i,j-1] + V[j]

for k = 1 to n-1
  for i = 0 to n-2
    MCV[i,i+k] = S[i,i+k] -
min{MCV[i+1,i+k],MCV[i,i+k-1]}
```

Question 68. Most Valuable Path (in Life)

Given a *n x m* grid filled with non-negative numbers, find a path from bottom left *(1,1)* to top right *(n,m)*, which maximizes the sum of all numbers along its path. You can only move either up or right at any point in time.

Solution

We can solve the problem using dynamic programming

1. Notation: Let $mvp[i][j]$ represent the maximum sum achievable from cell (i, j) to the top-right corner (n,m). We are interested in finding $mvp[1,1]$

2. Optimality: The principle of optimality holds in this case because any sub path of a maximum valued path must itself be a maximum valued path.

3. Recursive Call: For each cell (i, j), the maximum path sum $mvp[i][j]$ is computed based on whether the movement is to the right or upward. Thus, the recursive relation is: $mvp[i][j] = grid[i][j] + max\{mvp[i+1][j], mvp[i][j+1]\}$

   Base Cases:
   a. The value at the top-right corner $mvp[m][n]$ is initialized to the value in the grid at that position: $mvp[n][m] = grid[n][m]$

b. If you're on the right most column *(i = n)*, you can only move up, so: *mvp[n][j] = grid[n][j] + mvp[n][j+1]*

c. If you're on the top row *(j = m)*, you can only move to the right, so: *mvp[i][n] = grid[i][n] + mvp[i+1][n]*

4. Algorithm: Start filling the table from the top-right corner and proceed leftward along the top row and downward along the rightmost column. Afterward, use the recursive relation to fill in the rest of the table.

By following this approach, *mvp[1][1]* will eventually hold the maximum sum of the path from the bottom-left corner to the top-right corner.

We observe that the same algorithm can also be used if the question asks for the minimum valued path. The problem can also be phrased as maximum sum path, minimum sum path, etc.

Question 69. Diameter of a Graph

Diameter of a graph is defined as the largest distance between any pair of vertices of G. Give an efficient polynomial algorithm to find the diameter of the graph.

Solution

Diameter of a graph can be simply computed as first calculating all pairs shortest paths in $O(n^3)$ time, and then taking the maximum over all the n^3 values.

Question 70. Maximum Value Contiguous Subregion

You are given a two dimensional array $A[1:n, 1..n]$ of real numbers (possibly containing both positive and negative real numbers). You want to find a rectangular sub-region of the array that maximizes the sum of that region. For example, the subarray $S(1,2,5,8)$ consists of contiguous rectangle between $A[1,2]$ to $A[5,8]$, both corners inclusive, therefore, it has 35 total numbers. Give the most efficient polynomial algorithm for this problem that you can.

Solution

There are $O(n^4)$ sub-regions of the array to consider, which can be observed using the different indexes of the S notation. Further, to calculate the sum of any of these sub regions would take $O(n^2)$ time individually, but the sums of all these sub-regions together can be computed in $O(n^4)$ time total.

We use the following two notations.

Suppose $V(i,j)$ denotes the sum of all values from $(0,0)$ to (i,j). Clearly all n^2 values of $V(i,j)$ can be calculated in $O(n^2)$ time. Using the $V(i,j)$, each S value can be calculated in $O(1)$ time as follows.

$$S(i,j,k,m) = V(k,m) - V(k,j-1) - V(i-1,m) + V(i,j)$$

Therefore, the maximum value contiguous sub-region can be computed in $O(n^4)$ time.

Question 71. United Colors of Neighborhood

You are given a sequence of houses $1, 2, ... n$, and the cost to color those houses in k colors, using a 2-dimensional array: $C[1..n,1..k]$. $C[i,j]$, where $1 \le i \le n$, and $1 \le j \le k$, represents the cost to color the i-th house using j-th color. You want to minimize the cost to color all the houses, but with the constraint that no two neighboring houses should receive the same color.

Give the most efficient algorithm that you can for this problem.

Solution

Notation

Let $T(i,j)$ represent the minimum cost of coloring up till i-th house, such that the i-th house is colored using the j-th color.

Recursive Formulation

T(i,j) can be computed by minimizing over all color combinations till the *j*-th house that do not finish in the *i*-th color and then using the *i-th* color for the *j*-th house. Therefore, we can write the recursive formulation as follows.

$$T(i,j) = \min_{h \in \{1..k\},\ h \mathrel{!=} j} \{ T(i-1,h) + C(i,j) \}$$

The base case of this can be established as *T(1,j) = C(1,j)* for all values of *j*.

Proof of Optimality

We can easily prove using contradiction that if *T(i,j)* is optimal, then the constituent *T(i-1,j)* values must be optimal as well.

Algorithm

```
// Init. 1 indexing, ignore 0-index values
double[][] T = new double[n+1][k+1];

// Base case
for j = 1 to k
  T[1][j] = C[1][j]

for i = 2 to n
  for j = 1 to k
    T[i][j] = Infinity // Initialize
    for h = 1 to k such that h != j
      T[i][j]  =  min(T[i][j],T[i-1][h]  +
C[i][j])
```

Each entry $T(i,j)$ can be computed in $O(k)$ time. Since there are a total of $O(nk)$ values, the overall algorithm takes $O(nk^2)$ time. The same can also be observed from the three nested loops in the algorithm.

Question 72. Box Stacking Problem

You are given a set of n types of rectangular 3-D boxes, where the i-th box has height h_i, width w_i and depth d_i (all real numbers). You want to create a stack of boxes which is as tall as possible, but you can only stack a box on top of another box if the dimensions of the 2-D base of the lower box are each strictly larger than those of the 2-D base of the higher box. Of course, you can rotate a box so that any side functions as its base. It is also allowable to use multiple instances of the same type of box.

Solution

Firstly, we simplify the problem by getting rid of the rotation of boxes, by simply generating all combinations from the given type of box. Therefore, given i-th box of dimensions (w_i, d_i, h_i), we generate the following boxes for our problem:

(w_i, h_i, d_i)

(w_i, d_i, h_i)

(d_i, w_i, h_i)

(d$_i$, h$_i$, w$_i$)
(h$_i$, w$_i$, d$_i$)
(h$_i$, d$_i$, w$_i$)

Therefore, given *n* types of boxes, we generate *m =
6n* boxes for our maximization problem. We
consistently use the first two dimensions as width
and depth, and the third dimension as the height.

We sort the sequence of *m* boxes by the first
dimension and use the following variation of Longest
Increasing Subsequence.

Notation

Let *MH(i)* denote the maximum height that can be
generated using boxes *1..i*, such that *i*-th box is
definitely used.

Recursive Formulation

Recursive formulation can be obtained by
conditioning over all values of *j < i*, such that $d_j < d_i$.

$$MH(i) = max\ j < i\ |\ d_j < d_i\ \{MH(j) + h_i\}$$

Algorithm

The algorithm operates simply by generating all *MH*
values in $O(n^2)$ time, and then taking the maximum
over all values of *MH(i)* for all values of *i*. Therefore,
the entire algorithm runs in $O(n^2)$ time.

Question 73. Pseudo Polynomial Partition

Given a set consisting of n positive integers $[a_1, a_2, \ldots a_n]$, you want to partition into two parts so that the sum of the two parts is equal. Suppose $s = a_1 + a_2 + \ldots + a_n$. The time complexity of your algorithm should be $O(ns)$ or better.

[**Note:** Due to the presence of the term s in the time complexity, such an algorithm is called pseudo polynomial algorithm.]

Solution

We observe that the question regarding whether or not a partition exists is equivalent to asking whether or not there is a subset of numbers that add up to $s/2$. This is the more general formulation that we use to solve the partition problem. This alternative formulation is usually referred to as the **subset sum** problem.

Notation

We use a boolean variable $B(j,m)$ to denote whether or not a subset with a sum of m can be constructed using some numbers selected from $[a_1, a_2, \ldots a_j]$.

Recursive Formulation

We can construct a subset with a sum of m' from numbers selected from $[a_1, a_2... a_{j+1}]$ in two different ways. We either use a_{j+1} or we don't.

$$B(j+1,m') = max \{B(j,m'-a_{j+1}), B(j,m')\}$$

Therefore, we can compute each entry in the dynamic programming table in a constant amount of time. There are a total of $O(ns)$ entries in the table.

Once the entire table is computed, we only need to inspect if $B(n,s/2)$ is 0 or 1.

This dynamic programming algorithm runs in $O(ns)$ time.

Section 6:   Graph Traversal and Backtracking

Question 74. Edge Classification

Refer to the classification of edges, wherein edges are classified as "Tree Edges", "Back Edges", "Cross Edges" and "Forward Edges".

1. What types of edges can be found in a depth first search traversal of an undirected graph? Specifically, why can a forward edge not exist in a depth first search traversal of an undirected graph?
2. What types of edges can be found in a breadth first search traversal of an undirected graph?
3. What types of edges can exist in each of those cases if we consider directed graphs?

Solution

When we traverse an undirected graph using DFS, we can only encounter tree edges or back edges. It is not possible to see cross edges or forward edges, because of the very nature of DFS. If were to come across a cross edge *(u,v)*, where the vertex *v* has already been discovered, then that means that we would have traversed this edge from *v* and *(v,u)* would have become a tree edge. Similarly if *(u,v)* was classified as a forward edge where the vertex *v* has already been discovered, then also, we would have traversed this edge in the other direction *(v,u)* as a tree edge.

In the breadth first search traversal of an undirected graph, we can encounter tree edges, back edges and also cross edges. However, we cannot encounter any forward edges because due to the nature of BFS, if an edge *(u,v)* was a forward edge, then *v* would be discovered first through *u*, and therefore *(u,v)* would have become a tree (discovery) edge.

In the case of directed graphs, all edges are possible, as the edges cannot be traversed in both directions. Specifically, in case of DFS on directed graphs, we can encounter tree edges, back edges, cross edges as well as forward edges.

In the case of BFS on directed graphs, we can encounter tree edges, back edges and cross edges. However, we still cannot encounter forward edges for the same reason as described earlier, that if an edge *(u,v)* was classified as a forward edge, then that means that vertex *v* would have been discovered directly through *u*, and not through a descendent of *u*.

Question 75. Cyclic and acyclic graphs

A graph is called acyclic if it does not have any cycles. Prove that a directed graph is acyclic if the depth first traversal of the graph does not yield any back edges.

Solution

We can prove this claim using contradiction. Let us assume for the purpose of contradiction, that the given directed graph G is acyclic, and the DFS traversal of a directed graph G yields a back edge (u,v). Then, that implies that there is a path from v to u. That path combined with the back edge (u,v) constitutes a cycle in the graph G. This contradicts the assumption that G is acyclic.

Therefore, if the DFS traversal of a graph does not yield any back edges, then the graph G is acyclic.

Question 76. Topological Sort

Given a directed acyclic graph $G = (V,E)$, a topological sort T is an ordering of vertices, such that, for each directed edge (u,v) in E, u comes before v in T.

a. Prove that if the exploration of node u is completed before the exploration of node v in a depth first search traversal of G, then there exists a topological ordering in which u comes before v.

b. Using the above proof, modify the DFS algorithm to produce a topological ordering that adds vertices to a list as their exploration is finished.

Solution

Suppose we are given a directed acyclic graph $G(V,E)$, with an edge (u,v) where u comes before v. We observe from the previous question that because G is a DAG, there can be no back edges in G.

a. In a DFS traversal of G, if node u is visited before node v, then node u must be an ancestor of node v since there are no back edges. Therefore, there must be at least one directed path going from node u to node v that will have (u,v) in topological order. QED

b. The DFS algorithm can be modified in the following way to produce a topological sort of the vertices:

Consider that vertices can are white (unvisited), gray (pushed on the stack), or black (popped off the stack). Vertices will become black in reverse topological order. So to sort in topological order fill in an array in reverse order from the end with the nodes as they become marked black (popped off the stack).

Question 77. Finding a node whose deletion doesn't create large subtree

When you delete a non-leaf node of a tree, you create more than *1* subtree. Given a tree with *n* nodes, give an algorithm to find a non-leaf node *v*, such that deletion of node *v* leaves no subtree with more than *n/2* nodes.

Solution

When we use DFS traversal on a graph that is itself a tree, we only encounter tree (discovery) edges, and further, we can count the size of a subtree rooted at a node simply by counting the DFS number. Using this observation, we adjust the DFS algorithm as follows to identify a node *v* such that deletion of *v* does not leave a subtree with more than *n/2* nodes.

```
select a random node as the root of the DFS
traversal

for each node u
  for each child node x of u
    count size of each subtree rooted at x

number of nodes in the "parent" subtree = n
- sum of subtrees of all child nodes - 1
```

```
if number of nodes in each subtree of u ≤
n/2
    return u
```

Question 78. Finding all bridges in a graph

Given an undirected graph G, an edge *e* is called a *bridge* if deletion of the edge *e* disconnects the graph. Modify the algorithm that uses DFS to find all articulation points in a graph in $O(n + m)$ time to also find all the bridges in $O(n + m)$ time.

Solution

Articulation points and bridges can be found together in a graph using the same DFS based algorithm described in text. Consider a tree edge *(u,v)* in the DFS traversal of the graph *G*. Using the *L* and *DFN* values described in the text, the vertex *u* is a single point of failure with respect to child node *v*, if $DFN[u] \leq L[v]$, and edge *(u,v)* is a bridge if $L[v] > DFN[u]$.

Section 7:   Branch and Bound

Question 79. Minimum   Cost   Job   Assignment using B&B

You are given a two-dimensional $n \times n$ array where $a[i][j]$ represents the cost when the *i-th* worker is assigned *j*-th job. Any worker can be assigned to perform any job, but it is required to perform all jobs by assigning exactly one worker to each job and exactly one job to each worker in such a way that the total cost of the assignment is minimized.

Solution

We model the solution space as a graph, where each vertex represents the assignments that have been made. The root of the graph contains an empty assignment, that is, no jobs have been assigned to any worker.

This root node has *n* child nodes, and each branch can be interpreted as the job done by the first worker.

The graph can be visualized as follows.

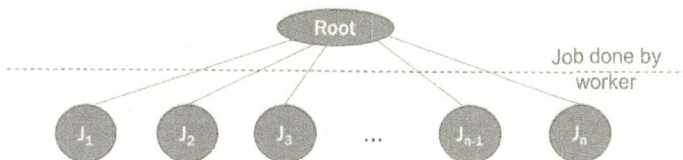

For each node in the solution graph, we can derive both upper and lower bounds on the assignment cost.

The upper bound can be a trivial assignment.

To derive a lower bound, we observe that:

- Each job must be done – so if we add minimum cost per job, then that must be minimum cost
- Each person must do a job – so if we add minimum cost per resource, then that must be minimum cost
- Taking the maximum of these two minimums, is a good "lower bound".

Once we have a lower bound on each node and an upper bound on each node, nodes for which the lower bound exceeds the upper bound of another node can be safely eliminated from further consideration. Other nodes can be expanded (branched) further.

Question 80. Applying Branch and Bound to TSP

How can we apply B&B to Traveling Salesperson Problem? Define how the solution space is modeled as a graph. Further, define lower and upper bounds on a node. Consider two cases: (i) The original problem is based on a graph in Euclidian space and therefore satisfies the triangle inequality, and (ii) The original problem does not satisfy the triangle inequality.

Solution

Suppose the graph consists of nodes $\{v_1, v_2, ... v_n\}$. To use the branch and bound to Traveling Salesperson Problem (TSP), we model the solution space as a graph. The root of the graph is defined as the part where no decisions have been made. Without loss of generality, suppose the TSP tour starts and ends at node v_1. The child node of the root denotes the node that follows v_1 in the traveling salesperson tour.

Upper and lower bounds

Since TSP is a minimization problem, the upper bound is a known solution. A known solution can be constructed using an in-order traversal of a Minimum Spanning Tree. A lower bound can simply be the weight of the minimum spanning tree.

With or without triangle inequality

If the triangle inequality holds, then TSP cannot be more than twice the cost of the MST. Therefore, the algorithm is guaranteed to produce a solution with cost that is no more than twice that of the optimal cost.

If the triangle inequality does not hold, then no such claim can be made.

Question 81. Applying Branch and Bound to SAT

You are given a Boolean formula involving variables $X_1, X_2, \dots X_n$. The Boolean formula is of form (C_1 AND C_2 AND C_3 ... AND C_m), where each clause is a disjunction (logical "or" function) of the X variables. You have to assign true/false values to the variables so as to maximize the number of clauses that evaluate to true. Present a branch and bound approach for this optimization problem.

Solution

Solution space can be created in the form of a rooted tree. The root node is where no decision has been made as to the truth value assignment to any of the n variables.

From the root node, we create two child nodes, around the selected variable X_i (how a variable may be selected is specified a bit later). One child node is when the selected variable is set to true, and the other one represents when the selected variable is set to false.

Each child node then leads to another child node where a different variable is selected. It can be observed that the height of the tree is n, and there are 2^n leaf nodes. This confirms that in the worst case, the branch and bound algorithm can run in exponential time. However, as in other cases, practically, we will be able to prune large portions of the tree which results in a time complexity that is significantly smaller.

Bounds

The given problem is a maximization problem. Therefore, the lower bound will be a known feasible solution, and the upper bound will be a theoretical bound.

At each node, based on the choices that have already been made, certain clauses are already set to true, and similarly, certain other clauses may have already been set to false. For the remaining clauses, a simple greedy algorithm can be used to count the number of clauses that be set to true. Therefore, lower bound (which represents a feasible solution) can be found in $O(n)$ time.

Upper bound is simply the number of clauses that are either true or not known to be true or false. (Or, in other words, the upper bound is n minus *the number of clauses set to false).*

Ordering Criteria

Like many other branch and bound algorithms, while the overall structure of the algorithm may be the same, it is the ordering criteria that makes a significant difference in the execution time practically. We suggest ordering the variables in order of their "incidence" count – the number of times a variable exists across all the clauses, minus the number of times it's complement exists across all the clauses.

Question 82. Branch and Bound Algorithm for Vertex Cover Problem

Given a graph $G = (V, E)$, a vertex cover (sometimes node cover) of a graph is a set of vertices such that each edge of the graph is incident on at least one vertex of the set. We are interested in finding the vertex cover of minimum size. Present a branch and bound approach for this optimization problem.

Hint: Consider any vertex v in V, either v is in the vertex cover, in which case we can delete the node v, and all edges incident on v from consideration. If the vertex v is in NOT the vertex cover, in that case, clearly all the neighboring nodes of v must be in the vertex cover. Use this argument to develop bounds for the B&B strategy.

Solution

We observe that Vertex Cover (VC, for short) is a minimization problem. Therefore, for this problem, the lower bound will be a theoretical bound, and the upper bound will be a known (feasible) solution.

Solution space can be created in the form of a rooted tree. The root node is where no decision has been made regarding any of the n vertices, as to whether the vertex is in the Vertex Cover or not.

From the root node, we create two child nodes, around the selected vertex v_i. One child node is when the selected vertex is included in the vertex cover, and the other child node represents when the selected vertex is *not* included in the vertex cover.

Each child node then leads to another child node where a different variable is selected. It can be observed that the height of the tree is n, and there are 2^n leaf nodes. This confirms that in the worst case, the branch and bound algorithm can run in exponential time. However, as in other cases, practically, we will be able to prune large portions of the tree which results in a time complexity that is significantly smaller.

Lower and Upper Bounds

At each node, based on the choices that have already been made, certain vertices are already in the vertex cover, and other vertices have already been deleted. Therefore, for an upper bound, a simple greedy algorithm can be used.

The lower bound can simply be the number of vertices that have not been eliminated from the graph.

Ordering Criteria

Like many other branch and bound algorithms, while the overall structure of the algorithm may be the same, it is the ordering criteria that makes a significant difference in the execution time practically. We suggest ordering the variables in order of their degree. That is, start with the highest degree vertices first.

Section 8: NP-Completeness

Question 83. Reducing Clique to Vertex Cover

Show a polynomial time reduction from the Clique problem to the Vertex Cover problem.

Solution

We observe that if a graph G has a clique of size k, then obviously the complement graph G' has an independent set of size k. Therefore, G' has a vertex cover of size $n-k$, where n is the number of vertices in G.

Therefore, the following reduction is sufficient.

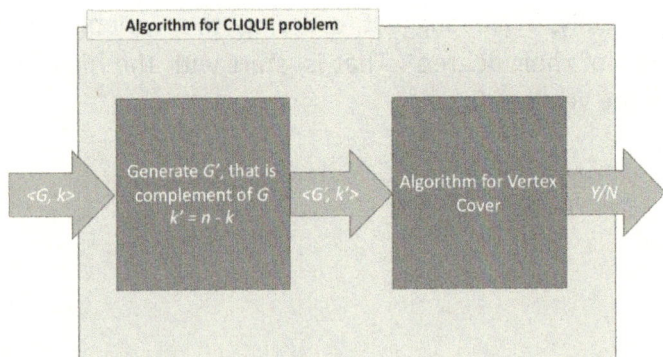

Using this reduction, we observe that if we have an efficient algorithm for the vertex cover problem, we can also solve the clique problem efficiently. Specifically, since the transformation routine runs in polynomial time, if (hypothetically) algorithm for vertex cover runs in polynomial time, then we have an algorithm for clique problem that runs in polynomial time also. In other words, CLIQUE $\leq_P$ VC, and vertex cover problem is at least as hard as the clique problem.

Question 84. NP-completeness of Dominating Set Problem

Given a graph $G = (V, E)$, a dominating set for the graph G is a subset D of V such that every vertex not in D is adjacent to at least one member of D. The "Dominating Set" problem is defined as given a graph G and an integer k, to determine if the graph G has a dominating set of size k. Prove that the Dominating Set problem is an NP-complete problem. (Hint: Show a reduction from Vertex Cover problem to the Dominating set problem.)

Solution

We start with a block diagram that shows the reduction from Vertex Cover to Dominating Set problem.

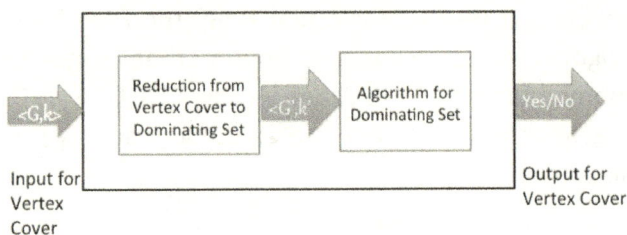

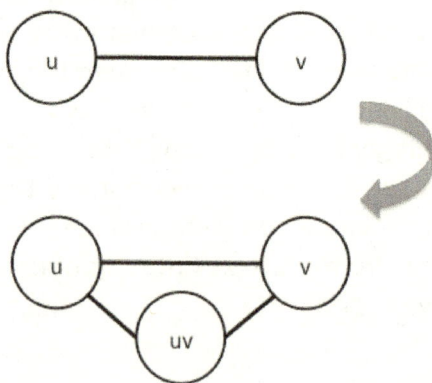

Figure 1: Reduction from the vertex cover to the dominating set problem.

Given an input <G, k>, we need to construct a graph G', such that G' has a dominating set of size k' if and only if G has a vertex cover of size k.

We assume that the given graph is connected. If the graph is not connected, the same reduction as described below can be applied on each connected component of the graph.

The intuition behind our reduction is that for vertex cover, we need to cover all the edges, while for dominating set, we need to cover all the vertices (either by selecting them, or by having them as neighbors).

This suggests the following transformation. For each edge (u, v) in G, we add a new vertex: uv, and add the edges (u, uv), (uv, v) and also keep the edge (u, v). In other words, we replace each edge with a triangle.

Now the claim is that if G has a vertex cover of size k, then G' must have a dominating set of size k, and vice versa. Since (u,v) is an edge in G, one of u or v must be in a vertex cover. Correspondingly, one of u or v must be in a dominating set in G'.

Question 85. Degree Constrained Spanning Tree

Finding a Spanning Tree is an easily solvable polynomial time problem. Consider a "k-degree constrained Spanning Tree", wherein we have to find a spanning tree such that no vertex in the spanning tree has degree more than k. Show that the k-degree constrained spanning tree problem is NP-complete.

Solution

If in a tree, the maximum degree is 2, then the tree is simply a path. This allows us to observe that the problem of finding spanning tree where no vertex has degree more than 2 is equivalent to finding a Hamiltonian path.

Therefore, the k-degree constrained spanning tree problem is simply a generalization of the Hamiltonian Path problem. Specifically, Hamiltonian Path problem can be directly reduced to the k-degree constrained spanning tree problem by leaving the original graph unchanged and simply using the value of k = 2.

Question 86. Long Simple Cycle

Prove that the following problem is NP-complete: Given a graph G, and an integer k, find whether or not graph G has a simple cycle consisting of k edges.

A simple cycle is defined as one that does not have any repeating vertices.

Solution

A cycle consisting of n edges is a Hamiltonian cycle. Therefore, the problem of finding a simple cycle of k edges is a generalization of Hamiltonian Cycle. The reduction diagram can be drawn, simply by instantiating the value of k to be n.

Question 87. Coloring is fun, but hard

Show that the problem to decide if a given graph G is 4-colorable is NP-complete. (Hint: Show a polynomial time reduction from 3-coloring to 4-coloring.)

Solution

Given graph G, we can construct a new graph G' that has one additional vertex, and that vertex is connected to all vertices of G. Then, G is 3-colorable if and only if G' is 4-colorable.

That is, 3-COLOR problem reduces to 4-COLOR in polynomial time.

Question 88. Coloring is hard, even within a range

The chromatic number $\chi(G)$ of an undirected graph G is the minimum number of colors required to color the vertices, so that adjacent vertices have different colors. Computing the chromatic number exactly is NP-hard, because 3-Color is NP-hard. Prove that the following problem is also NP-hard: Given an arbitrary undirected graph G, return any integer between $\chi(G)$ and $\chi(G) + 5$.

Solution

Consider a graph G. For the purpose of contradiction, we assume the presence of a coloring algorithm that can color the graph G using x colors, such that $\chi(G) <= x <= \chi(G) + 5$. Now, we create a graph H, such that it consists of *10* copies of G. Every vertex in a copy of G is connected to every vertex in all other copies of G. If the graph G has *n* vertices and *m* edges, the graph H has *10n* vertices, and *10m + 90n* edges. We observe that we can use the coloring algorithm to color H using *y* colors, and that $\chi(H) \leq y \leq \chi(H) + 5$. Since H just has *10* copies of G, and because every copy must use its own set of colors, $\chi(H) = 10\,\chi(G)$. Therefore, we have that $10\,\chi(G) \leq y \leq 10\,\chi(G) + 5$. That is, $\chi(G) \leq y/10 \leq \chi(G) + \frac{1}{2}$. Since $\chi(G)$ is an integer, we have computed the $\chi(G)$ exactly. Since computing the chromatic number is NP-Hard, approximating the chromatic number within additive factor of 5 must be hard as well.

A similar proof can be built for any additive factor.

Question 89. Long chain of friends

You are given a list of people, and statements of the form "x knows y". You are asked to find, is there a chain of k people, such as x_1 knows x_2, x_2 knows x_3, and x_{k-1} knows x_k. Prove that this problem is NP-complete by using one of the known NP-complete problems (CLIQUE, 3-SAT, Hamiltonian Path, Hamiltonian Cycle, Independent Set, etc.)

Solution

A chain of friends that is of length n is essentially a Hamiltonian Path. Therefore, the "long chain of friends" problem is a generalization of the Hamiltonian Path problem. The reduction diagram can be drawn from Hamiltonian Path to "Long chain of friends" problem by instantiating the value of $k = n$.

Question 90. Discovery of the Sun

A sun graph looks like a circle, with a hanging vertex on each vertex on the loop. The problem to discover the sun is defined as follows: Given a graph G, identify, is there a sun graph inside the given graph *G*, such that all vertices of graph *G* are in the sun graph?

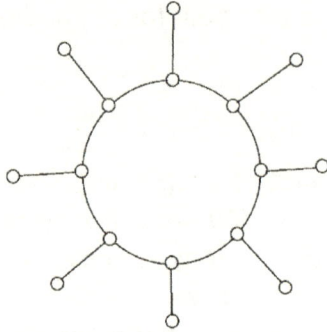

Prove that this problem is NP-complete using any of the known NP-complete problems as a starting point.

Solution

Other than the vertices on the periphery of the sun, the cycle is a Hamiltonian cycle on the remaining vertices.

This observation allows us to reduce the Hamiltonian Cycle problem to the Discovery of the Sun problem in the following manner.

Given a graph *G* with *n* vertices, we construct a new graph *G'* by adding *n* new vertices and connect each new vertex a corresponding old vertex. Clearly, *G* has a Hamiltonian cycle if and only if G' has a sun graph inside that spans all the vertices of G'.

Question 91. Improved Algorithm for Maximum Independent Set

Consider the Maximum Independent Set problem. Show an optimal algorithm for this problem that runs in $o(2^n)$ time.

Solution

We make the following observation about the independent set with respect to any vertex v. Either the maximum independent set contains the vertex v or it does not. If it does not, then we can simply remove the vertex. If it does, then we can remove that vertex and all its neighbors and the find the maximum independent set in the remaining graph. This observation can be used to design a divide and conquer algorithm that runs in better than $O(2^n)$ time, where n is the number of nodes in the graph.

The recurrence relation for the two cases is:

$T(n) = T(n-1) + T(n-2) + 1$

This recurrence relation leads us to time complexity that is $O(\phi^n)$, where ϕ is the golden ration, approximately equal to *1.6*.

This algorithm can be further improved by only looking at vertices of degree at least 2. Firstly, we observe that in a graph G, if a vertex is of degree 0, then it can simply be included in the independent set. Also, if the vertex is of degree 1, then also it can be included in the independent set and the neighboring vertex discarded. Therefore, after such preprocessing is done, we can have a graph where there exists a vertex with degree at least 2. When the vertex of degree 2 is considered, the time complexity in that case becomes:

$$T(n) = T(n-1) + T(n-3) + 1$$

This leads to an even more efficient algorithm.

Section 9: Theory of Lower Bounds

Context

For the following problems, the objective is to prove or disprove a certain lower bound. It is worthwhile to note that lower bounds apply to a specific computation model. There are three *common* computation models, although there are many other important ones as well. The three common computation models that we consider are:

- Simple decision tree: In this model, we can compare two numbers (such as two different elements of an array) and then branch based on the outcome

- Linear decision tree: In this model, we can compare a linear function (involving more than one variable, such as different elements of an array) and then branch based on the outcome.

- Algebraic decision tree: In this model, we can compare a polynomial function of degree d (involving more than one variable, such as different elements of an array) and then branch based on the outcome.

Question 92. Partial Sorting of Array

Consider the usual sorting problem: given an array A, we want to sort the array. The twist now is that we don't want to sort the array completely. Rather, we want to sort the array into k blocks so that each block of numbers is larger than the numbers in the previous block. In other words, the array is partially sorted. Prove that any comparison based sorting algorithm that solves this partial sorting problem must require $\Omega(n \log k)$ time.

Solution

Given n numbers, we can have $n!/((n/k)!^k)$, that is, $O(k^n)$ outputs. Therefore, the height of the decision tree must be at least $n \log k$.

We observe that as a trivial example, if $k = n$, that is there are n blocks of size 1 each, the lower bound translates to the familiar $\Omega(n \log n)$ lower bound.

Question 93. Min and Max

Prove that minimum and maximum of an array cannot be found that in less than $3n/2 - 2$ comparisons in worst case.

Solution

We prove that for any given algorithm *A*, there is a sequence of numbers for which *A* takes at least *3n/2 − 2* comparisons to find both the maximum and minimum numbers. Such a proof can be constructed with an adversary argument, in which the adversary thinks in terms of numbers in *three* states. First state contains numbers that have not yet been compared to anything. Second state contains numbers that have only won or lost games that they have played. So, they are candidates for being the maximum (or the minimum). Finally, the third state contains numbers that have both won and lost games they have played. So, they are not candidates for being the minimum or the maximum.

Initially all *n* numbers are in the first state. The adversary ensures that a maximum of two numbers move from first state to second state during each comparison, and during this comparison, no number goes into the third state. Further, the adversary ensures that during each comparison, a maximum of one number enters the third state, and in those comparisons, no number leaves the first state. So, we observe that we need *n − 2* comparisons simply to fill up the third state and we need at least an additional *n/2* comparisons just to empty out first state. Therefore, in total, we need to make at least *3n/2 − 2* comparisons just to make sure numbers and their states have the desired sizes before algorithm A can draw its conclusion.

Question 94. Element Distinctness

Given an array containing n elements, we want to identify if there is a duplicate element in the array. Prove that this problem must require $\Omega(n \log n)$ time.

Solution

We consider a linear decision tree model. The crux of the argument is as follows. We consider the space of all inputs, that is, each number is in R, that is, the overall input is in R^n. While the overall set of inputs is uncountably infinite, we are merely interested in identifying uniqueness as the output. Therefore, we think of the input as $n!$ connected components, one for each permutation (in terms of sorting). For each permutation, there is an uncountably infinite set of values in domain that belong to the same permutation and has the same outcome. Considering a linear decision tree model, after every comparison involving the linear function, we divide the domain into possibly 3 more sub-regions (corresponding to the 3 different outcomes, less than, equal to or greater than). That is, we can reach a maximum of 3 times more candidate decisions. Finally, when the algorithm is finished, we need to be able to reach a total of $n!$ decisions. Thus, any decision tree that determines uniqueness has $n!$ leaves, and therefore, the height of the decision tree must be $\Omega(n \log n)$.

We observe here that the core argument depends on the number of connected components, and this argument can be applied to other problems as well. A seminal work in this field is (Ben-Or, 1983). Another related work is (Dobin & Lipton, 1979).

We further observe that if we simply counted the number of *distinct* outcomes, that is only *2* (either the array has a duplicate element, or it doesn't). Therefore, an argument that simply counts the number of distinct outcomes can be used to prove that the lower bound on time is at least *log (2)*, that is, *1*. This lower bound obviously has slack in it, as the other lower bound above demonstrates.

Section 10:   Graph Theory

Context

Many questions in this section involve the concept of vertex and edge coloring. A vertex coloring of a graph is labeling the graph vertices with different labels (or "colors"), such that adjacent vertices do not receive the same label/color. Similarly, a proper edge coloring of a graph is an assignment of labels (colors) to the edges of the graph such that adjacent edges do not receive the same color. Coloring problems are inherently minimization problems, since we can always color a graph with n distinct colors, one for each vertex. Therefore, the objective usually is to use as few colors as possible.

Vertex Chromatic (or Edge Chromatic) number is the minimum number of colors needed for a proper vertex (or edge) coloring.

Question 95. High Density Two Colorable Graph

Give an example of a graph that contains **at least** 6 vertices, and each vertex has **at least** 4 neighbors, and the graph has a valid vertex coloring using only 2 colors.

Solution

A graph *G = (V,E)* is said to be bipartite, if it's vertex set *V* can be divided into two subsets V_1 and V_2, such that, for every edge *e* $\in E$, one end points of *e* is in V_1 and the other end point is in V_2. We observe that a bipartite graph requires only *2* colors, one for vertices in V_1 and the other color for vertices in V_2. A bipartite graph can be made highly dense, for example, if we have *10* vertices in V_1 and *10* vertices in V_2, and each vertex in V_1 is connected to each vertex in V_2, then degree of each vertex is *10*, there are *100* edges for *20* vertices, and yet, the graph only requires *2* colors for a valid vertex coloring.

Question 96. Triangle Free Graph Requiring 4 Colors

Give an example of a graph that has the following properties. (Note that you need to give a single graph as the answer.)

(i) The graph does not contain a triangle (that is, a clique of *3* vertices) as a subgraph.

(ii) Graph needs at least *4* colors for a proper vertex coloring

Solution

Such a graph can be constructed as follows.

We start with a cycle on 5 vertices, that is a C_5: $\{v_1, v_2, v_3, v_4, v_5\}$. This graph is an odd cycle, and it needs 3 colors. This graph does *not* contain a triangle.

The description below assumes that the addition operation is 1 indexed and is modulo 5. That is, $5 + 1 = 1, 3 + 4 = 2$, etc. For every $<v_i, v_{i+1}, v_{i+2}>$ in C_5, add two more vertices x_i and y_i, such that $v_i, v_{i+1}, v_{i+2}, x_i$ and y_i also comprise a C_5.

We can observe that the graph constructed so far, can also be colored using 3 colors.

Now, we add 20 more "z" vertices. Each vertex is connected to one of x_i and one of y_j such that $i \neq j$.

After including these 20 new "z" vertices, we have a total of 35 vertices, and the graph constructed so far, can also be colored using 3 colors.

We are now ready to add a new vertex that will require the 4-th color. This new vertex w is connected to ALL 20 "z" vertices. Clearly, this vertex must use a different color, and by construction the entire graph is still triangle free.

We observe that the entire construction is based on creating a set of vertices that use all 3 colors and are not connected to each other at all. Those are the "z" vertices.

The construction presented above is not the smallest such graph with the desired properties, but it serves as a useful example with a deliberate construction.

Question 97. Hamiltonian Path, but No Hamiltonian Cycle or Articulation Point

Given an example of a graph that has a Hamiltonian Path, does not have any articulation point, and does not have a Hamiltonian cycle. If you claim that such a graph is not possible, prove this claim.

Solution

This is clearly possible. Graph in Figure 2 shows this possibility.

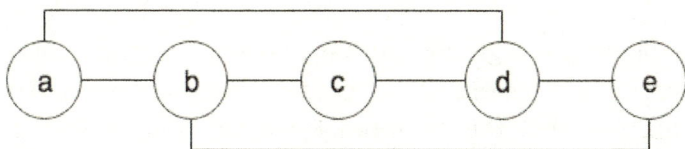

Figure 2: A graph that has a Hamiltonian Path, but has no Articulation Points and no Hamiltonian Cycle.

Question 98. An Instance of Vizing's Theorem

Give two graphs, such that, both the graphs have the highest degree as 3. One graph should have a valid edge coloring with *3* colors, and other graph should require *4* colors for a valid edge coloring.

Solution

A graph which has maximum degree *3* and requires *3* colors for a proper edge coloring is straightforward. Clearly, each of the *3* edges needs a distinct color.

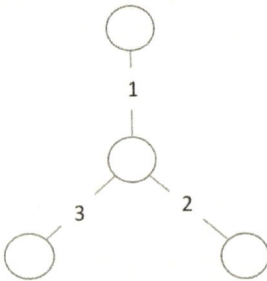

Following is a graph that has maximum degree *3* and requires *4* colors for a proper edge coloring. To observe that this is optimal, we can start with the edges around the central vertex of degree *3*. The three edges can be labeled as *1, 2* and *3,* without loss of generality. This forces the colors of the other edges as well.

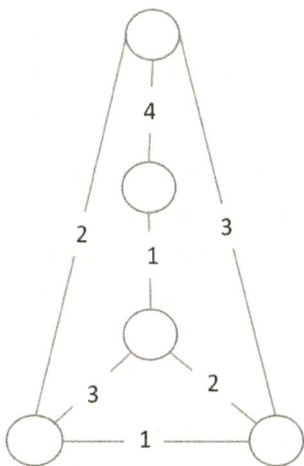

These two graphs give an illustration of Vizing's Theorem, which states the following. For a graph G, such that the maximum degree is Δ, the edge chromatic number is either Δ or $\Delta + 1$.

Question 99. Matchings in Bipartite Graphs

Let $G = (V, E)$ be an undirected graph. A matching M in G is a subset of edges $M \subseteq E$ such that at most one edge is incident to each vertex in V. We are interested in finding a matching of highest cardinality. Clearly, the maximum possible size of a matching is $V/2$.

A graph $G = (V,E)$ is said to be bipartite, if it's vertex set V can be divided into two subsets V_1 and V_2, such that, for every edge $e \in E$, one end point of e is in V_1 and the other end point is in V_2.

Matchings can be constructed by building a sequence of *augmenting paths* where an augmenting path a path in which the edges belong alternatively to the matching and not to the matching and starts from and ends on two vertices that are not covered by the matching.

Given a bipartite graph, give an $O(nm)$ algorithm to find the maximum matching.

Solution

The central idea of augmenting path-based algorithms is to start with an uncovered vertex, that is, a vertex that is not in the current matching, and traverse a path such that we finish at another vertex that is not in the current matching. Such an augmenting path can be found in $O(m)$ time. Once we find an augmenting path, we switch all the vertices that are in the augmenting path – the ones that were in the matching are no longer in the matching, and the ones that were not in the matching are now added to the matching. After an augmenting path is found, the size of the matching increases by 1. An example augmenting path is shown in Figure 3.

Starting with an empty matching, we can only find a maximum of $min\{|V_1|, |V_2|\}$ augmenting paths. Therefore, we can find the maximum matching in a bipartite graph in $O(mn)$ time.

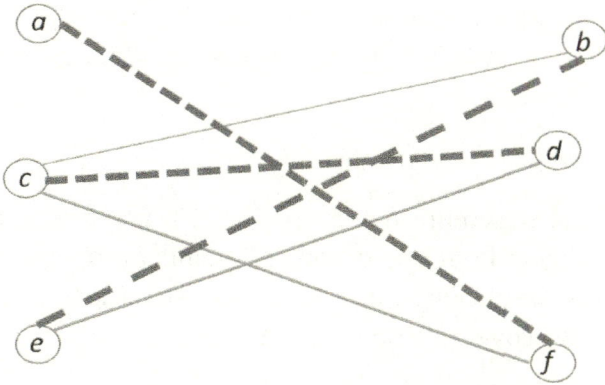

Figure 3: Augmenting Path <a,f,c,d,e,b> can be used to extend the exist matching {{c,f}, {e,d}}

Question 100.   Matchings   and   Vertex Covers

A vertex cover of an undirected graph *(V, E)* is a subset $S \subseteq V$ such that, for every edge $e \in E$, at least one of end points of *e* lies in *S*. Prove that in every graph, the minimum size of a vertex cover is at least the size of a maximum matching. Further, give a non-bipartite graph in which the size of a minimum vertex cover is strictly bigger than the size of a maximum matching.

Solution

If the maximum matching size in a graph is *x*, then clearly at least one of the end points of the matching must be included in a vertex cover. Therefore, the vertex cover must be at least *x*.

A simple triangle graph as shown in Figure 4 provides an example where the size of the minimum vertex cover is strictly larger than the size of a maximum matching. As can be easily observed, the size of the minimum vertex cover is *2*, while the maximum matching is only of size *1*.

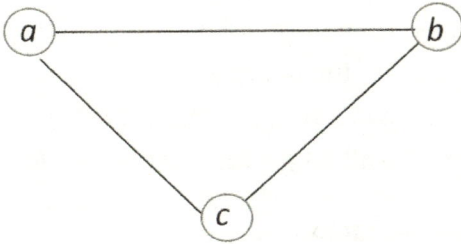

Figure 4: A graph where minimum vertex cover is of size 2, and is strictly larger than the size of maximum matching, which is 1.

Question 101.　　Minimum Vertex Cover on a Graph

(New topic: This problem introduces the concept of approximation algorithms)

Given a planar graph G = (V, E), find the minimum vertex cover in linear time. As described earlier in the chapter on branch and bound algorithms, a *vertex cover* A vertex cover of an undirected graph *(V, E)* is a subset $C \subseteq V$ such that, for every edge $e \in E$, at least one of end points of *e* lies in *C*. The minimum vertex cover is the vertex cover with the smallest possible size.

Solution

This can be done using a simple greedy strategy:

- Start with an empty vertex cover.
- While there are edges remaining, pick an arbitrary uncovered edge *(u, v)* and add both *u* and *v* to the vertex cover.
- Remove all edges incident to *u* or *v*.

Approximation Factor:

Consider the set of edges picked by the algorithm. The optimal cover must pick at least one vertex from each edge in the graph, and specifically, for each edge picked by the algorithm.

- Let C^* be the optimal vertex cover and C be the cover produced by the greedy algorithm.
- For each edge, there is at least one corresponding vertex in the optimal vertex cover C^*. Since the algorithm picks both vertices per edge, $|C| \leq 2 |C^*|$.

Bibliography

Arora, A. (2016). *Analysis and Design of Algorithms* (Vol. 3rd). Cognella Academic Publisher.

Ben-Or, M. (1983, April). Lower bounds for algebraic computation trees. *Proceedings of the Symposium on Theory of Computing, 15*(http://doi.acm.org/10.1145/800061.80873 5), 80-86.

Dobin, D. P., & Lipton, R. J. (1979, Feb). On the complexity of computations under varying sets of primitives. *Journal of Computer and System Sciences, 18*(1), 86-91.

Index

About the Author

As a faculty member in the Department of Computer Science at the George Washington University, Prof. Arora teaches graduate and undergraduate courses in computer science, mostly related to design and analysis of computer algorithms and artificial intelligence. Dr. Arora is also the author of the book "Design and Analysis of Algorithms" published by University Readers and Cognella Academic Publishing.

As part of his industry experience, Dr. Arora is the co-founder and Chief Executive Officer at ClayHR, the leading software for human capital management software. At ClayHR, Dr. Arora has led the company to many successful product launches and numerous customer acquisitions.

Dr. Arora has also served as AVP – Product Management at Edifecs Inc., VP – Solutions at hCentive, Inc. and VP – Technology at NTELX, Inc. As part of the Affordable Care, Dr. Arora designed WebInsure Exchange Manager, a leading product in the $200 MM market for connecting insurance companies (payers) to the public health insurance exchanges. As a leading expert in risk targeting, Dr.

Arora led the technical design for US FDA's PREDICT system which currently screens more than 52 million imports a year.

Dr. Arora's efforts in supporting FDA's PREDICT program were recognized by the FDA commissioner Dr. Margaret Hamburg. The transportation management system designed by Dr. Arora for the port of Aqaba in Jordan won the award for most innovative product given by Intelligent Transportation Society of America.

Dr. Arora earned an undergraduate degree in Computer Science and Engineering from the Indian Institute of Technology, Delhi (IITD) and masters and doctorate degrees, both in Computer Science, from the George Washington University (GWU). He enjoys spending time with his family, hiking in the mountains, and is an avid museum goer.